# SAM THE COOKING GU[...]

## AND THE

# HOLY GRILL

# SAM THE COOKING GUY

## AND THE

# HOLY GRILL

## Easy & Delicious Recipes
## for Outdoor Grilling & Smoking

# SAM ZIEN

**Countryman Press**

*An Imprint of W. W. Norton & Company*
*Independent Publishers Since 1923*

Manufacturing by TC Transcontinental
Book design by Allison Chi
Production manager: Devon Zahn

Countryman Press
www.countrymanpress.com

An imprint of W. W. Norton & Company, Inc.
500 Fifth Avenue, New York, NY 10110
www.wwnorton.com

978-1-68268-801-4

10 9 8 7 6 5 4 3 2 1

HERE'S WHAT THE
COVER ALMOST
LOOKED LIKE

# THANK YOU

**KELLY**—for being the best part of me, for as long as I can remember.

**ANN**—for believing in me again (even though you hated my subtitle).

**LEIGH**—for keeping me centered, on track and out of trouble.

**LUCAS**—for your photography and creativity—I wouldn't do this with anyone else.

**JILL**—for always being there ready, with a smile and the ability to find what I'm looking for.

**GREG & MATT**—for being gracious enough to write "blurbs" for the back of the book. But at the time I wrote this page, I hadn't see them yet, so I hope they're aren't shitty and mean. In any case, thank you both.

**BUT, A MOST IMPORTANT THANK YOU TO ALL OF YOU WHO SUPPORT ANYTHING I DO**—you'll never know how much it means.

# CONTENTS

# INTRODUCTION

**THE EARLIEST FORM** of cooking was done outside. A group of cave people (persons?), sitting around a roaring fire, roasting brontosaurus ribs or pterodactyl wings. Grunting, laughing, and—let's be honest—probably ruining their food. And save your breath, because it's already been pointed out that cave people and dinosaurs did not exist at the same time—but it makes for a better intro.

In fact, my own early days at the grill were also spent undercooking, overcooking, and blackening food—and not in a good way. And though we've all progressed since then (me included), the concept of cooking over fire was always a solid one. We know almost all food just tastes way better outside—that's a given. And when you combine that with the social aspect of cooking and entertaining out there—it's simply a great time. Everyone loves cooking in nature—even if nature is merely your backyard. And this includes my YouTube audience as well. I know that because out of our top ten most-watched videos, six have been grilling or barbecuing episodes with more than 40,000,000 views.

Even so, given the choice of having to grill or use the stove, many people would choose inside because they think it's easier. But for many reasons, that's just not true.

Outside, the cleanup is easier, because there are seldom pots or pans.

Outside, there's virtually no splatter—and if there is, it's outside.

Outside, there are no smoke alarms to set off.

Outside, you won't heat up your house.

Outside, energy costs are minimized.

Outside, over fire or smoke is one of the healthiest ways to cook. Because excess fat and grease from whatever you're cooking falls through the grates to the flames or charcoal below, so the meat is never just sitting in it.

Outside, that fat and falling grease create smoke, and the smoke creates amazing flavor.

I hope, at this point, you're convinced. But I won't stop there, because we're going to show you pretty much anything you need to be successful outside. We're gonna kick the fear of grilling right the eff outta you, and answer some important questions along the way.

One thing, though: If you're looking for a book dedicated solely to using Texas post oak in an offset stick burner to improve your chances at a KCBS event—this book is definitely not for you. Sorry, let me translate:

**TEXAS POST OAK:** the preferred wood of many when it comes to smoking meats in Texas

**KCBS:** Kansas City Barbeque Society, the largest competitive barbecue organization in the world

**STICK BURNER:** a smoker designed to cook meat, using only logs that have been split into smaller "sticks" as opposed to charcoal or pellets

But . . . if you want to expand your outdoor game in all areas, have more fun, learn some new recipes, and generally get more comfortable cooking delicious food at the grill or smoker, I'm here for you and have your back. So relax, keep reading, and get ready to become the master of your (outdoor) domain.

# Q & A

I get asked many of the same questions all the time, so let's answer them.

### What's the difference between grilling and barbecuing?

It's a good question, especially when you consider how often we use the terms interchangeably:

"I'm going outside to grill these steaks."

"I'll be back in a few; it's time to throw this chicken on the barbecue."

And while they clearly both refer to food that's cooked outside, they generally mean two different things.

Grilling is typically cooking food directly over higher heat, often with the lid up, and usually over gas, charcoal, or briquettes. Grilling generally happens quickly.

Barbecuing is mainly cooking your food low and slow with the lid closed, over some kind of wood or charcoal—smoking, essentially. And then, it's often larger cuts of meat: full briskets, pork shoulders—that kind of stuff. Barbecuing can take anywhere from 6 to 16 hours.

Think of it like this: You go to San Antonio for barbecue, but you go to your cousin Neil's house for burgers and dogs on his grill.

Of course, there are exceptions to everything, but in general, that's kind of it. And while this book has a chapter dedicated to smoking, most of the recipes will be about grilling over gas or charcoal, etc. But some items can go both ways, and when they can, I'll tell you. We like options.

### Gas vs charcoal—which one is right for me?

It pretty much comes down to convenience vs flavor. When I first started grilling, I never wanted to wait for charcoal to light, so I almost always used my gas grill. You fire it up, close the lid, and in about 10 minutes, it's ready to go. But whenever I cook over charcoal, I'm reminded how much more flavor has been added. Take heart, though—there is a way to get that charcoal flavor without its taking forever, or having the charcoal go out on you—it's called a "charcoal chimney starter," and it changed everything for me. You can read all about it when you get to the "Equipment" section.

### Lump charcoal or charcoal briquettes?

Lump charcoal is simply wood that's been burnt in an oxygen-starved environment until it's essentially pure carbon. It burns hotter than briquettes, but that means it also burns quicker, so you can end up using more. And it's more expensive than briquettes. On the plus side, it doesn't leave much in the way of ash. The only thing that really annoys me about lump is, you almost always end up with a bunch of small, crumbly pieces that are nearly impossible to use.

Charcoal briquettes, on the other hand, have that uniform, cute little pillow shape. They're not pure like lump and, for sure, contain additives that are not necessarily a bad thing—unless you're all about that. They can take longer to light than lump, so use a chimney and who cares? And even though they create more ash than lump (which must be cleaned up, obviously) they're definitely cheaper than lump.

And there's also this—you can pretty much find briquettes anywhere.

So, what's the upshot? Unless you're a Texas pitmaster getting ready to compete in a barbecue championship somewhere . . . use what you like. I go between both, and am never disappointed.

### Is lighter fluid a good thing to use when lighting your grill?

No, and in fact, it never was. I realize plenty of people use it, but they shouldn't because it's gross, smelly, and made from chemicals. And the same goes for "match light" charcoal or briquettes, because they've been soaked in lighter fluid—ewww. But there are natural fire starting options, like small tumbleweed-looking things or pressed blocks. Even a cooking oil–soaked paper towel will work beautifully. Plus I've already told you about the chimney, so just forget the stinky stuff.

### How do I keep food from sticking?

Ah, yes, the age-old question. There are two things to know:

1. Cook on a clean grill. I know it seems obvious, but clean means really clean. Because those stuck-on, leftover little bits of chicken or beef will definitely not help. So, do this: When it's time to cook, preheat your grill well with the lid closed for 10 to 15 minutes first. This will not just help it get to a proper cooking temperature, but will then make it easier when you use a grill brush to get off the bits from your last cooking session.

2. Lubricate your grill. There are two schools of thought here. The first is to use a rag, or a few layers of folded paper towel, dipped in oil and brushed on the grates. Sorry, but I find that a pain. So, once the grill is hot, and I've cleaned it, I use cooking spray right before I put on any food. Would the KCBS guys approve? Guessing not. Am I concerned? Nope. So, look for the line "Clean and oil the grill grates" at the start of recipes. And by oil, I mean a spray, of cooking oil or anything you choose to grease it down with.

### When should I add a BBQ sauce?

This is an easy one. For any sauce with a high sugar content, you always wait to add near the end. Too early, the sugars will burn, and you don't want that. Notice, though, I said, "near the end," not "at the end." And that's because you want to let the sauce start to caramelize a bit on what you're cooking, which will require the heat. I start painting it on in the last few minutes of cooking, and then one last time when I take the food off the grill.

### How to tell when food is done without cutting into it?

For starters, if you can help it (and you can), try not to cut into what you're cooking. But here's the real answer: Get your hands on an instant-read digital thermometer. I talk about this more in the "Equipment" section, but trust me here—it'll change everything. And for God's sake, don't employ the "pushing on parts of your palm to determine doneness." Because unless you've been cooking in a restaurant forever, and understand how different cuts will feel differently when you push on them, you'll ruin more stuff than you want. Oh, and if you have mastered the push—great. Just please don't email to tell me how good you are.

### What's two-zone cooking, and why is it important?

Boy, am I glad you asked, because this is very important. Two-zone cooking is a simple concept whereby you set up your gas or charcoal grill with a "hot" side and an "indirect" side. The beauty is that you start off searing on the hot side, then move your food to the indirect side to continue cooking with an even level of heat, as in an oven—without burning. Think of a thick chicken breast or steak—yes, you could cook it only on the hot side, but doing it this way will give you a much better product when you're done. Remember it like this: "Sear on the hot, finish on the not." Okay, I know that's a dumb line, but now that you've read it, you can't unread it and will remember.

To set up your grill for two-zone cooking:

- A two-burner gas grill: preheat the grill with both burners on, but before you put on the food, turn off one side.
- A three-burner gas grill: preheat the grill with all burners on, but turn off the middle one before putting on the food.
- Four burners or more: this is probably a big, expensive grill, which means you likely have someone to cook for you. Just have them do it.

- A charcoal grill: build your fire, but keep it pushed over to one side of the grill. They even sell charcoal baskets that let you simply move them where you need them.

## An Important Note about Cooking Times

Regardless of what I say in this book—or what any author in any cookbook says—cooking times will vary based on many factors. Food temp, outdoor temp, grill temp, how often you're lifting the lid, etc. So use timing in recipes as a guide, combined with a thermometer, and you'll be fine.

SMOKED & WRAPPED PORK RIBS (PAGE 165), GOES-WITH-ANYTHING COLESLAW (PAGE 227)

# EQUIPMENT

There are really only two things you need for outdoor success:

**SPRING-LOADED TONGS:** It's about control. And a good pair of spring-loaded tongs (not a long, bent piece of metal that pretends to be tongs) will let you do everything you need to during cooking. I prefer a short-handled 9-inch version for any flipping, holding, turning, etc. "But, Sam, what about a spatula or long grill fork?" you might be wondering. Anything you'd need a spatula for, the tongs will handle, and better. And before you try to make a case for needing a spatula when flipping burgers, I'll say that when a patty is ready to be flipped, it's firm enough for the tongs. And forget forks—they just poke holes in whatever you're cooking and let juices out.

**INSTANT-READ DIGITAL THERMOMETER:** Again, it's about control and a digital thermometer removes the guesswork when determining doneness. And I say digital, because they read much faster than the analog type—like, in less than 5 seconds vs 15 to 20. And while saving a few seconds may not seem like a big deal, keeping your smoker or grill lid open longer because of an analog thermometer to check the temperature of something, will only serve to drop the entire temperature way down and it will take that much longer to recover. Plus, you can get a reliable one for less than $25. If I'd only had one of these when I was first learning to grill. Come to think of it, they weren't around then, so never mind.

But using one correctly is important, and here are a few rules:

- You want to start checking before the end of your estimated cooking time. You can always keep cooking if it's not done enough. But if it's too done, you can't fix it.
- The probe should be inserted into the thickest part and through to the center, from the top for larger cuts.
- The probe should not touch any bone, as that will give you a false reading.
- You should definitely check more than one spot—and if one end is cooking faster than another, just turn around what you're cooking
- Expect some amount of "carry-over cooking." That simply means a protein will continue cooking while it rests, and can rise maybe another 5ish degrees.

**COOK TO TEMP, NOT TIME:** Just because I say, for example, "cook for about an hour, or until 145°F" doesn't mean pull it off at an hour exactly. The time estimate is just a guide, and cooking to the temp is more important.

With only good tongs and an instant-read thermometer, I could cook almost anything. But here are a few other items that will make your outdoor life potentially easier and much more delicious.

**OVEN DIAL THERMOMETER:** While we're in thermometer territory, let's talk about this one. It has a 2-inch dial and is designed to sit or hang in an oven. But here's where it's great: It lets you determine the ambient temperature inside your gas grill, so you can use your grill like an oven. The Twice-Smoked Sweet Potatoes (page 68) are great in the smoker, but if you don't have one, you could use your grill, with less smoke, of course, but still. And this thermometer will let you know the temperature, exactly. Oh, I'd be remiss if I didn't mention that there are digital versions of thermometer, but they cost a bunch more money and I don't need to do that to you.

**CAST-IRON PAN:** I use mine outside, on my grill, constantly and for a variety of things: mussels, smoked cream cheese, French onion mac & cheese, bone marrow, steaks, and the list goes on. Oh, and by "mine," I mean my Sam the Cooking Guy 12-inch cast-iron pan (shameless plug, I know, so feel free to check out ShopSTCG.com to get yours). But not only does cast iron pretty much last forever, it can literally take the heat, because cast iron melts at somewhere around 1,500°F, and we're not getting close to that. You've heard of "farm to table"; well, this is "grill to table," because you cook in it and then serve in it.

**REVERSIBLE FLAT GRIDDLE:** Usually cast iron or cast aluminum, the flat side let's you use your grill for pancakes, eggs, etc. I mostly use the ridged side on the stove in my kitchen to get great grill marks on stuff.

**GRILL BASKET:** I love this thing. It's a perforated metal pan with high sides that lets you cook small foods on the grill without their falling in between the grates, but still lets them benefit from the flames and smoke below. Wanna stir-fry a bunch of shrimp? It's perfect. How 'bout a big pile of onions and peppers for a sandwich? Yup. Even a piece of fish will cook better in one. Oh, and you can pick one up for as little as $15.

**GRILL BRUSH:** We've talked of the importance of keeping your grill clean, and that's where a grill brush comes in. But I'm going to encourage you to get a bristle-free version, which is still wire, but set as a continuous coil, rather than in individual bristles like a toothbrush. The problem with metal bristles is they can dislodge from the brush head, and end up in your throat with a bite of grilled chicken—and that only ends badly.

**CHARCOAL CHIMNEY STARTER:** The concept is really simple: You just fill the chimney with charcoal, put some crumpled newspaper or a couple of fire starters in the open area at the bottom, light it, and voilà—efficiency at its greatest. And in less than 30 minutes, when the coals on top are covered with gray ash, it's go time. Plus, since you should take proteins out of the fridge about 30 minutes before going to the grill, you have the perfect time to ready your charcoal.

**SMOKER BOX:** This smart little guy gives you the ability to add smoke flavor when using a gas grill. It's a stainless-steel box that you fill with wood chips, then set it above the flames. And when the box heats, the chips smoke, and boom—smoky food. You're not getting a level of smoke as you would in a proper smoker, but then, you're only paying about $15, not $500+.

Now, let's talk about what to cook on. There are many choices here, and I'll cover the key ones:

**GAS/PROPANE GRILLS:** We all know these and have likely used them a jillion times. You turn the dial, an electric spark hits the gas, they flame up, and in about 10 minutes, you're cooking—they're as easy as it gets in the grilling world. They can start at around $200 (with small ones even closer to $100) but then go as high as $12,000—yes, $12,000! As you probably can imagine, when the price goes up, so do the size, quality, and bells and whistles. But how much do you really need? If it's your first grill, read reviews and buy what you're

BISTECCA ALLA FIORENTINA
(PAGE 158)

comfortable spending, and don't get talked into anything crazy, because who knows how your cooking needs/style will change. And if you're buying a small one, try to get one with two burners so you can employ the two-zone cooking technique (see page 11).

**CHARCOAL GRILLS:** I know I'm not going to convince everyone to get on the charcoal train, but it's a delicious one you should think about:

- *Kettle Style:* Let's say you want to get into cooking on charcoal, but don't want to make a big spend of it, here's your answer. In fact, Weber still sells the one they've been making since the '50s—and it's near perfect. By managing your charcoal, you can use it for low and slow, or get it screaming hot for whatever you need. And get this: it can be yours for not much more than $100.
- *Barrel Smoker/Cooker:* Imagine a 30- or 50-gallon drum turned on its end. The charcoal goes in the bottom, and you cook by either hanging proteins like ribs, or laying such things as chickens or briskets on a rack. The temperature is regulated by opening or closing vents at the top and bottom. But the fact that you can hang a rack of ribs in the cooker, and after 3 or 4 hours they come out perfectly cooked and the bottom is no more done than the top . . . is beyond me. These can start at $200 and top out around $500 to $600. I like them a lot, but I wouldn't make one my only charcoal cooker, because you're mostly cooking low and slow on them.
- *Kamado:* Not mentioning any brand names, but these are the egg-shaped things you see all over. If you're looking for charcoal, this is a good option for a bunch of reasons. The first is that, because most are made of ceramic, they hold heat like crazy, and crazy means a long time, so you can use them for smoking. But they also excel at high heat, meaning you cook hot and

fast for steaks, etc. They're pretty easy to clean, last a long time, and are sturdy because they're ceramic. You can actually buy a little guy for a few hundred dollars, but can go up to $2,000 for a large one.

**SMOKERS:** There could be an entire book dedicated to this, but I'll try to keep it short. The category is really diverse and runs the gamut from the stick burner I already mentioned in the intro, all the way to the ultimate in plug & play smoking, the "pellet" smoker. I'm partial to these because once you fill it with pellets (compressed wood that looks like little rabbit shits), set the temperature, and put on your food, away you go. BTW, the pellets come in different wood options (hickory, mesquite, apple, pecan, etc.) to give you different flavors and levels of smoke. The upshot is you can put on a brisket or pork shoulder at midnight, and go to sleep. And the smoker will automatically add pellets to the firepot by itself throughout the night to maintain the temperature. As opposed to a stick type that has you getting up to add wood, etc. If you want to get into smoking, this is a great way to do it. The downside, if there is one, is that they give a lighter level of smoke flavor than the other type—which for me is just fine. A smallish fellow will start around $400, and they can climb up to close to $4,000.

A few other things before I turn you loose:

**READ:** Read the recipes all the way through first. This is always a good idea, and makes sure you know what's coming up.

**OIL:** In a recipe, "oil" always means a neutral oil and preferably one that can handle high heat, such as avocado, peanut, or even canola. Olive oil and its more expensive cousin "extra-virgin" are not in this category. I'll specify that when I want you to use it.

**SALT:** For cooking, I always use kosher salt, for a few reasons. One, it's natural with no additives. Two, the grains are large and coarse, making for more even seasoning. For finishing though, I'll sometimes use a flaky sea salt.

**AND FINALLY, TRY THINGS YOU NORMALLY WOULDN'T:** I'm always saying, "Don't make the same things all the time," and I really mean it. Just because you always make your Aunt Clara's chicken on Tuesdays, doesn't mean you have to. No disrespect to Clara, but how about throwing in something different one Tuesday? If you're a carnivore, definitely scope out the chapter on beef, but maybe try something from another chapter first. The Tequila Lime Chicken Tacos (page 88) would be a delicious start. The point is, use the book and try new things. Got it? Cool.

Okay, no more talking—now we cook . . .

JUNIOR CARNIVORE

# RUBS, SAUCES & MORE

Think of these as "enhancers." You're already working with something great . . . a little chicken, some steak, even a piece of fish. But now a little sauce here, a rub there, or even a quick dip can change the whole game. And why shouldn't it? You're not here for the same thing, are you? If you always use a basic BBQ sauce on your ribs, maybe it's time to try the Alabama White? Or as you're finishing your steak, a few swipes of Joy's Steak Sauce sends you into a direction you weren't expecting. Not to get too deep, my friends—but that's life. Because, if you're not learning and trying new things, you're merely existing—and that's boring.

# ALL-PURPOSE RUB

As the name would imply, this can go on anything.

**MAKES ABOUT 1 CUP**

¼ cup kosher salt

1 tablespoon coarsely
ground black pepper

1 tablespoon garlic powder

1 tablespoon smoked paprika

1 tablespoon ground cumin

1 teaspoon onion powder

1 teaspoon crushed red pepper
flakes, for a little heat (optional)

1. Put everything in a small bowl and mix well.
2. Store in a tightly sealed container.

# SPG

This tends to be my go-to for things like steak and burgers—when I want the natural flavors to come through. Even the Texas-Style Beef Brisket (page 215) uses only this.

**MAKES ABOUT ¾ CUP**

½ cup kosher salt

¼ cup coarsely ground
black pepper

2 tablespoons granulated
garlic (not garlic salt!)

1. Put everything in a small bowl and mix well.
2. Store in a tightly sealed container.

SPG

CHIPOTLE BLACK RUB

ALL-PURPOSE RUB

SWEET HOT RUB

# CHIPOTLE BLACK RUB

A little smoky, a little spicy and midnight black—and what an impression it makes. Seriously great on anything, though probably best on beef because some might think black chicken is, well, horrific looking. In fact, check out the Hanging Tomahawk (page 197). Oh, and the charcoal powder is easily purchased online.

**MAKES ABOUT ¾ CUP**

2 tablespoons kosher salt

2 tablespoons chipotle chili powder

2 tablespoons coarsely ground black pepper

2 tablespoons granulated garlic

2 tablespoons onion powder

1 tablespoon food-grade activated charcoal powder

1. Put everything in a small bowl and mix well.

2. Store in a tightly sealed container.

# SWEET HOT RUB

Oh yes, my fave because it's a little of both. I use this on pork a lot, and it's fabulous. And lately, I've been sprinkling a little in my morning scrambled eggs . . . you almost can't go wrong using it with anything.

**MAKES ABOUT 1 CUP**

3 tablespoons light brown sugar

3 tablespoons chipotle chili powder

2 tablespoons ground cumin

2 tablespoons garlic powder

2 tablespoons smoked paprika

2 tablespoons kosher salt

1 tablespoon coarsely ground black pepper

1. Put everything in a small bowl and mix well.

2. Store in a tightly sealed container.

# SWEET & SMOKY BBQ SAUCE

The very first ribs I ever cooked on television used a simplified version of this sauce. It contained BBQ sauce, syrup, and brown sugar. It's just better now with a little punch from the vinegar, and rich smokiness from the chipotles. If you're sensitive to heat, maybe start with one chipotle—you can always add more.

**MAKES ABOUT 2 CUPS**

1½ cups plain, store-bought BBQ sauce

¼ cup pure maple (or pancake) syrup

¼ cup light brown sugar

1 tablespoon white or cider vinegar

1 to 2 tablespoons minced chipotle chiles

1. Combine everything in a small bowl and mix well.
2. Store in an airtight container in the refrigerator.

# JOY'S STEAK SAUCE

My mom could grill a steak better than almost anyone, anywhere—it was crazy. This sauce, and how she used it, was the key. Because she didn't use it for serving on the side, like you would with a regular steak sauce—though you're certainly welcome to. it was mostly for brushing on a steak a couple of minutes before she pulled it off the grill. She passed away at an amazing 96 years, but it wasn't until this book that I started thinking about this damn sauce. And after a little tinkering, I think I got pretty close.

**MAKES A LITTLE MORE THAN 1 CUP**

½ cup plain BBQ sauce

3 tablespoons Cholula hot sauce

2 tablespoons prepared yellow mustard

2 tablespoons olive oil

1. Combine everything in a small bowl and mix well.
2. Store in an airtight container in the refrigerator.

JOY'S STEAK SAUCE

ALABAMA WHITE BBQ SAUCE

CAROLINA MUSTARD SAUCE

SWEET & SMOKY BBQ SAUCE

# CAROLINA MUSTARD SAUCE

Ribs often get the same treatment but deserve more. This sauce is sweet and tangy, with a touch of heat—damn.

**MAKES ABOUT 2 CUPS**

¾ cup prepared yellow mustard

⅓ cup honey

¼ cup light brown sugar

2 tablespoons hot sauce
   (I'd use Cholula here)

2 tablespoons soy sauce

1 tablespoon garlic powder

Kosher salt and freshly
   ground black pepper

1. Combine all the ingredients in a small saucepan, mix well, and let come to a very small simmer over medium heat. Continue to cook, stirring often, until the brown sugar has dissolved, 4 to 5 minutes.

2. Remove from the heat and let cool to room temperature. Then, store in an airtight container in the refrigerator.

# ALABAMA WHITE BBQ SAUCE

White BBQ sauce is not what you think of reaching for when at the grill. But it's so interesting in look and taste—you should. It's a little sweet, a little sour, and has a little bite from the horseradish—it's a hit on all levels.

**MAKES ABOUT 1 CUP**

¾ cup mayonnaise

3 tablespoons prepared
   horseradish

2 tablespoons cider vinegar

1 garlic clove, minced

Juice of ½ lemon

1 teaspoon sugar

1 teaspoon coarsely
   ground black pepper

½ teaspoon kosher salt
   (smoked, if you have it)

1. Combine everything in a small bowl and mix well.

2. Store in an airtight container in the refrigerator.

# JERK SAUCE

Let me say this first: This is definitely not the prettiest sauce in the book, or anywhere, honestly. But that will more than be made up for by its taste. Jerk seasoning is the Jamaican spice blend that can be used on almost anything—shrimp, pork, fish, and yes, chicken. It's hot from the habaneros, but tamed down by the brown sugar, and is something you'll want again and again. But while the Jamaican is typically a dry spice version, this is a wet marinade, and just know when using it on pork or chicken (such as the Jerked Chicken Legs, page 85), it is best to marinate overnight. Seafood needs only a few hours.

**MAKES ABOUT 1 CUP**

1 bunch green onions, white and light green parts, cut into 1-inch pieces

5 garlic cloves, peeled

One 1-inch piece fresh ginger, peeled and cut into slices

2 habanero peppers, stemmed and chopped roughly

½ yellow onion, diced

¼ cup light brown sugar

2 teaspoons ground allspice

2 teaspoons ground ginger

2 teaspoons dried thyme

1 teaspoon ground cinnamon

1 tablespoon kosher salt

Juice of 1 lime

Juice of 1 lemon

1 tablespoon Worcestershire sauce

¼ cup neutral oil

¼ cup water

1. Put everything in a blender and blend until smooth.

2. Use, cuz you'll be really happy when you do.

# BASIL PESTO

Pesto—what isn't it good for? And if you like it a little spicy, add the serrano. And if you need a little inspiration, I use it on the Italian Elote (page 63) and the Grilled Eggplant Parm (page 67). And here's a thought—an Italian Benedict with pesto instead of hollandaise, and prosciutto or capicola instead of Canadian bacon? Now we're thinking.

**MAKES ABOUT 1½ CUPS**

2 cups packed fresh basil leaves

¼ cup pine nuts

2 garlic cloves

½ cup grated Parmesan

1 serrano pepper, stemmed, seeded, and roughly chopped (optional)

½ cup extra-virgin olive oil

Kosher salt and freshly ground black pepper

1. Put the basil, pine nuts, garlic, Parmesan. and serrano (if using) in a blender or food processor.

2. Blend continuously until finely chopped.

3. With the blender running, slowly drizzle in the olive oil until well combined.

4. Add salt and black pepper to taste and start using right away, or seal well and refrigerate. The flavors will just get better as it sits.

# GREEN & RED CHIMICHURRI

Chimichurri, an uncooked herb sauce, is the darling of Argentinean grilling. It's insanely delicious on steak, fish, and chicken, but also on grilled veggies. And why only have one sauce, when you can both? The red is lesser known, but definitely no less delicious.

**MAKES ROUGHLY 1 CUP OF EACH**

GREEN
4 garlic cloves, peeled
½ cup olive oil
1 bunch parsley, leaves and finer stems only (I like curly parsley)
2 tablespoons chopped fresh oregano leaves
2 tablespoons red wine vinegar
Juice of 1 lemon
½ teaspoon kosher salt
½ teaspoon ground cumin
¼ teaspoon crushed red pepper flakes

RED
3 large garlic cloves, peeled
1 large shallot, peeled and roughly chopped
½ cup loosely packed fresh parsley
½ cup loosely packed fresh cilantro
4 ounces jarred roasted red peppers
Big pinch each of kosher salt and freshly ground black pepper
1 teaspoon ground cumin
1 tablespoon smoked paprika
1 teaspoon red pepper flakes
2 tablespoons red wine vinegar
½ to ¾ cup olive oil

These instructions apply to either sauce, so . . .

1. Put all the ingredients for either in a blender or food processor* and whiz until well blended but still a little chunky.

2. Store in the fridge. Let come to room temperature before using.

*No processor or blender? Not to worry; you can simply chop everything really well by hand or mix in a mortar and pestle.

HOW ELSE TO USE CHIMICHURRI

# GARLIC WHITE SAUCE

Remember the Frank's RedHot tagline "I put that shit on everything?" Well, that's how I feel about this sauce. The Twice-Smoked Sweet Potatoes (page 68) are better because of it, and so is the HSP (page 81), the Grilled Cabbage (page 71), and of course, the Lamb-Stuffed Pitas (page 134). In fact, the fish tacos we serve at Not Not Tacos in San Diego have this on them. You could call this the little black dress of the book.

**MAKES ABOUT 1½ CUPS**

½ cup mayonnaise

½ cup sour cream

3 large garlic cloves, minced

1 teaspoon ground cumin

Juice of ½ lime

1 tablespoon finely chopped fresh parsley

1 tablespoon white vinegar

½ teaspoon kosher salt

¼ teaspoon coarsely ground black pepper

2 to 3 tablespoons milk

1. Put all the ingredients, except the milk, in a small bowl and mix well, then add a couple of tablespoons of milk to make it drizzle-able.

2. Store in an airtight jar in the refrigerator.

# CILANTRO SAUCE

I realize many people are not fans of cilantro, and some even believe they possess a "cilantro-hating gene." I even hated cilantro, myself, many years back, but realized that wasn't really an option if you lived in Southern California (cuz it's on everything). So, I learned to like it—and any haters should, too. Think about putting this on anything, like the Garlic White Sauce. Tacos love it, veggies love it, and so does the Beef Kofta (page 179).

**MAKES ABOUT 1 CUP**

⅓ cup sour cream

⅓ cup olive oil

Juice of 1 lime

2 garlic cloves, chopped roughly

¾ teaspoon kosher salt

⅛ to ¼ teaspoon red pepper flakes

1 large bunch cilantro

3 tablespoons milk

1. Put everything in a food processor or blender and whiz until smooth.

2. Put some on a spoon and delight at its deliciousness.

3. Then, store in the fridge in an airtight container.

CILANTRO SAUCE

GARLIC WHITE SAUCE

# ITALIAN DRESSING

You can literally open my fridge any time and will always find some of this. We eat a lot of salad, and this is easily our go-to. But also, a good dressing like this can be used many ways, including the Charred Parmesan Hearts of Palm (page 60) and Jill's Grilled Halloumi Salad (page 64). One more thought: The Chicken We Make All the Time (page 82) but without the pita part, diced and on top of any collection of salad greens with this dressing is an unbeatable combo.

**MAKES ABOUT 1 CUP**

¾ cup olive oil

¼ cup red wine vinegar

½ teaspoon kosher salt

¼ teaspoon freshly
  ground black pepper

1 large garlic clove, crushed

2 teaspoons Dijon mustard

1½ teaspoons
  Worcestershire sauce

1½ teaspoons dried oregano

1½ teaspoons soy sauce
  (optional but shouldn't be)

1. Put everything into a jar, deli container, dressing shaker, sock—anything you can shake and not have it spill all over you. Okay, so maybe a sock is a bad idea.

2. Shake until everything is mixed really well.

3. Use—like, right now; but if not, it'll be good stored in an airtight jar in your fridge for about a week.

# ROASTED TOMATILLO SALSA

Despite looking like a baby green tomato (which it is not) a tomatillo is my favorite when it comes to a salsa. It's also a fruit, generally a little more sour than a green tomato, and has a nice bite. And when it gets roasted, it becomes amazing. Make this and make it often.

**MAKES ABOUT 2 CUPS**

1 pound tomatillos (about 6 or 7)
4 large garlic cloves, not peeled
1 jalapeño pepper
1 serrano pepper
1 small white onion, cut
  into quarters
Neutral oil
¼ cup chopped fresh cilantro
Kosher salt

1. Heat a grill to medium-high or set the oven to BROIL.

2. Remove the paper husks from the tomatillos and rinse well to get off the sticky stuff.

3. Put the tomatillos, garlic, peppers, and onion in a bowl, then drizzle lightly with oil.

4. If you're grilling, put everything on a grill pan on the grill and start charring. If you're using the oven, put everything on a baking sheet, then place 6 to 8 inches under the broiler. The goal for either method is to get some really good charring all the way around—and that means flip the veggies over so both sides get the heat.

5. When you've achieved a lovely char, remove from the grill or broiler and let cool slightly.

6. Squeeze the garlic out of its skins into a processor or blender, and add the tomatillos, peppers, and onion. Whiz until nicely chunky, transfer to a bowl, and add the cilantro and salt to taste.

7. Use or store in an airtight jar in the refrigerator.

# APPETIZERS

Ever been looking at a menu in a restaurant and said, "Anyone want to share a few appetizers?" Well that's me, a lot of the time. But it's no different here, and I suggest you choose them all. The Caramelized Onion & Garlic Cheese Bread will own you. The stupidly named Italian Canoe will surprise you. And the Kokoda will have you yearning for the Fijian Islands. It's not more of the same, it's more of the WTF?

# GRILLED ARTICHOKES

It's easy to forget about these prickly, goofy-looking things in the supermarket. But they're so good, you shouldn't—and they make one of our favorite appetizers. Most of the time, they're just cooked in water before being eaten. And we'll do that, but then will finish them on the grill, and that just makes them better. And don't forget about the heart, because just as with people, it's the best part. Wait, that came out wrong, and a lot creepy . . .

**SERVES 2 TO 4**

½ cup mayonnaise
¼ cup sour cream
1 tablespoon curry powder
¼ teaspoon smoked paprika
2 large artichokes
½ lemon
⅓ cup olive oil
2 garlic cloves, minced
1 teaspoon salt
½ teaspoon coarsely
   ground black pepper

1. Combine the mayo, sour cream, curry powder, and paprika in a small bowl. Mix well, then set aside.

2. Bring a large pot of water to a boil.

3. Cut a small slice off the bottom of each artichoke stem to clean it up, cut off and discard the points off each leaf (to keep you and your guests from getting poked), then cut the artichokes in half lengthwise and immediately add to the boiling water. Cook for about 15 minutes, or until tender, then drain.

4. While they cook, squeeze the lemon juice into a medium bowl, add the olive oil, garlic, salt, and pepper, and stir to combine.

5. Brush both sides of the cut artichokes with the lemon oil, then place them cut side down on the grates of your grill.

6. Grill, turning often and basting with the lemon oil as you go, until they're a little charred (charring is good), maybe 5 to 10 minutes.

7. Serve immediately with the curried mayo like this: Grab the tip of one of the leaves, and pull it off the artichoke. The inner bottom of the leaf has about ¼ inch of artichoke meat on it. Dip that bottom part into the curried mayo, and use your teeth to sort of scrape the meat off the leaf, then just repeat and repeat.

8. When you get down to the "choke," the fuzzy inner leaves, scoop them off and discard. Then, enjoy what's left: the heart, dipped in the curried mayo.

# CARAMELIZED ONION & GARLIC CHEESE BREAD

There's garlic bread, there's cheese bread, there's garlic-cheese bread—and then, there's this. There is just something about deeply caramelized onions . . . that kind of puts me in a trance. In fact, I said, "This is the best garlic bread I've ever had" as I was taking my first bite. I just hope it was not out loud, because I was alone.

**SERVES 6 TO 8**

9 tablespoons (1 stick +
  1 tablespoon) butter,
  at room temperature

1 tablespoon olive oil

1 medium yellow onion, diced

2 tablespoons garlic paste, or
  6 garlic cloves, minced finely

½ cup shredded Parmesan

1 bunch green onions, white
  and light green parts
  only, chopped finely

⅓ cup chopped fresh curly parsley

1 teaspoon red pepper flakes

½ teaspoon kosher salt

1 French or sourdough baguette
  (don't tell the French,
  but I think sourdough is
  a better choice here)

1. Melt 1 tablespoon of the butter and the oil in a large skillet over medium heat, then add the onion.

2. Stir well so they all get a bit of a bath in the butter and oil, then cook, stirring often, until golden brown and caramelized, about 20 minutes. Remove from the heat and let cool a bit.

3. Put the remaining 8 tablespoons of butter, plus the garlic, Parmesan, green onions, parsley, red pepper flakes, salt, and cooled onions in a medium bowl and mix really well.

4. Set up grill for two-zone cooking, and try to maintain about a 400°F temperature.

5. Cut the baguette lengthwise and spread the butter nonsense on each cut side.

6. Place them buttered side up on the indirect side of the grill and close the lid. Keep a bit of an eye on it, but you're probably looking at close to 15 minutes—and depending how your grill is set up, you'll want to move the pieces around a bit so they all get even exposure to the hot side(s).

7. Then, simply remove from the grill, cut into serving pieces, and have at it.

# SMOKED TOMATO & ROASTED GARLIC SOUP

Tomato soup, by itself, is always great. Adding roasted garlic and a little chipotle chile to it makes it even better. Sneak in a little smoke, and it becomes something special. But take heart, my friend—no smoker, no problem, because you can do this in the oven just as easily. And for that touch of smokiness, check out the note that follows about liquid smoke.

## SERVES 4

4 pounds vine-ripened tomatoes, cored and cut in half—please don't use rock-hard tomatoes

1 large yellow onion, peeled, root end cut off and discarded, chopped into 6 to 8 pieces

Kosher salt and freshly ground black pepper

5 or 6 sprigs thyme

Olive oil

1 head garlic, with ½ inch cut off the top to expose all the cloves

1 tablespoon tomato paste

1 chipotle chile (the type in adobo sauce)

2 cups chicken stock

Liquid smoke (optional)*

Croutons and chopped parsley for garnish

*Liquid smoke really is made from smoke, which is captured by condensing the smoke from burning wood. It comes in a little bottle, because you only need a small amount. So, I'd start with ¼ teaspoon, and add more from there if you like.

1. Preheat a smoker to 425°F.

2. Put the tomatoes and onion on a baking sheet, season with salt and black pepper, top the tomatoes with the thyme sprigs, and drizzle everything nicely with 2 to 3 tablespoons of olive oil.

3. Put the garlic head cut side up on a doubled 8-inch square of foil, drizzle with a tablespoon of olive oil, and seal tightly, then add to baking sheet.

4. Smoke for 45 minutes, or until the tomatoes and onion have softened beautifully. Remove from the smoker.

5. Heat a large pot over medium heat. Add a tablespoon of olive oil and the smoked onion pieces to the pot—if they're already very tender, move on to the next step; if not, stir well for a couple minutes to let them soften more.

6. Add the smoked tomatoes. Add the smoked garlic by grabbing the head from the bottom (not the cut side) and squeezing the now gorgeously softened cloves right out of their skins. Add the tomato paste and chipotle chile, then stir for a couple of minutes and add the chicken stock. Mix well.

7. Bring to a boil to let the flavors combine, then either use an immersion blender to mix everything in the pot, or transfer to a stand blender or food processor and whiz until the soup attains your desired thickness. If you used a stand blender or processor, return the soup to the pot.

8. Simmer for about 20 minutes, or until reduced and slightly thickened. If using the liquid smoke, this would be the right time to add some.

9. Serve with croutons and chopped parsley and dive in.

# GRILL-GRILLED CHEESE WITH PROSCIUTTO

It occurred to me one day that a "grilled cheese" is, well, not actually grilled. It's maybe flat griddled, or panfried—but grilled? Not so much, and it's time to fix that. So, this little guy will be cooked right on the outdoor grill and will not just be delicious, but will go perfectly with shot glass–size servings of the Smoked Tomato & Roasted Garlic Soup (page 41). And if you're wondering how a grilled cheese becomes an appetizer, it gets cut down to smaller servings. I like having these ready to go on the grill when guests come over, and put someone else in charge of making them.

**SERVES 6 TO 8**

½ cup mayonnaise

1 large garlic clove, minced

2 garlic cloves, minced finely

12 ounces shredded cheeses—any kind really, but I like a combo of fontina, mozzarella, Monterey Jack, and Parmesan

8 slices bread of your choosing, though definitely something hearty like sourdough; I mean, it is going on the grill

2 vine-ripened tomatoes, sliced into 4 slices each

12 slices prosciutto

1. Preheat a grill to medium.

2. Combine the mayo and garlic well in a small bowl, then set aside.

3. In a separate bowl, mix the cheeses together if using multiple kinds, and build for each sandwich: the bottom slice of bread, about 1.5 ounces of the cheese, 2 tomato slices, 3 slices prosciutto, another 1.5 ounces of the cheese, and finally the top slice of bread.

4. Clean and oil the grill grates, brush the top slices of bread with the mayo mixture, and place mayo side down on the grill.

5. Cook until beautiful grill marks appear, turn 45 degrees and cook until more marks appear, then add more of the mayo mixture to the top and flip over.

6. Repeat until crispy, golden, and marked—4 to 5 minutes per side total.

7. Cut into shareable, smaller pieces.

# SMOKED CREAM CHEESE

The first time I heard of this, I thought it was a joke, I mean, c'mon—smoking cream cheese? And then I tried it. And I'm here to say it's no joke, truly delicious, easy, and so damn adaptable to almost any flavor profile you want. Serve this with some great crackers and a drizzle of hot honey—oh damn.

**MAKES ONE 8-OUNCE BLOCK**

One 8-ounce block plain
  cream cheese

2 to 3 tablespoons Sweet
  Hot Rub (page 22)*

*I used the Sweet Hot Rub, but it literally could be anything: everything bagel seasoning, just the SPG (page 20), Japanese *togarashi* for a spicy chile pepper kick—anything.

1. Preheat a smoker to 225°F.

2. Make ¼-inch-deep crosshash marks across the top of the cream cheese.

3. Sprinkle the rub evenly over the top and sides, then place the block of cheese in a small, heatproof pan (cast iron works great, plus looks great for serving, too).

4. Place on the smoker and say good-bye for 2 hours.

5. Remove and use, like, right now, Sparky, cuz it's so good.

# ITALIAN CANOE

This is a grilled version of a Turkish flatbread called a *pide* that's normally baked with different things stuffed inside. But if I called it that, not many people I know, other than my Turkish friend Alp, would know what the hell it was. So, I needed a catchy name that would get your attention, and voilà, the Italian Canoe was born. Is it a stupid name, probably. Is it delicious? Oh yes, it is. Plus, it's a fun appetizer to bust out for your company. What else could you ask for? Okay, maybe someone to make it for you, but other than that?

**SERVES 10**

1 tablespoon olive oil
½ cup any color onion, diced small
½ cup red bell pepper, diced small
1 French baguette, 18 to 20 inches in length
½ cup mayonnaise
1 cup shredded mozzarella
1 pound ground Italian sausage
SPG (page 20)
½ cup chimichurri, green or red (page 29)

1. Preheat a grill to medium-high. Clean and oil the grill grates.

2. Heat the oil in a skillet, and sauté the onion and pepper for 2 to 3 minutes, until they start to soften. Remove from the heat and let cool.

3. Slice the baguette lengthwise and pull out the doughy insides; save these for croutons or bread crumbs.

4. Spread the mayo across the bottom of each "canoe," then evenly scatter the onions and peppers across the bottom, top with the mozzarella (pushing it down), and finally, put in the sausage, squishing it down evenly all across each canoe. Season lightly with the SPG, then lightly brush the top of each with some of the chimichurri.

5. Gently place each canoe face down, diagonally, on the grill.

6. Cook for about 7 minutes, then carefully turn each 45 degrees and cook for another 5 minutes or so—obviously you're just cooking long enough for the sausage to be cooked through.

7. Flip over gently again and let them cook on their back for 3 to 5 more minutes.

8. Remove from the grill, brush with a little more of the chimi, and slice into 2-inch lengths.

9. Serve. Sometimes I wonder, if I didn't write "serve" as a direction, would people get to the end and wonder what to do next, as in, "Hey, now what?"

# GRILLED POLENTA BRUSCHETTA

I think firm polenta gets overlooked a lot, and this combination of it grilled, then topped with the cool, basil-y tomatoes and soft goat cheese, is a dream. And in the interest of not doing everything last minute, the tomato part of this can be made a day in advance (and should) cuz the flavors will just get way better.

**SERVES 6 TO 8 AS AN APPETIZER**

4 Roma tomatoes, seeded and diced small

2 tablespoons chopped fresh basil

1 large garlic clove, minced finely

1 tablespoon olive oil, plus more for grilling

Kosher salt and freshly ground black pepper

1 pound chub polenta (what a name, huh?)

1 cup soft goat cheese

1. Combine the tomatoes, basil, garlic, olive oil, and salt and pepper to taste in a small bowl. Mix well, then set aside.

2. Heat a grill to medium-high.

3. Slice the polenta (removing the rounded ends) into ¼-inch-thick slices.

4. Brush the slices lightly with the oil and grill on each side for 7 to 10 minutes, until they get really good grill marks.

5. Remove the beautiful little rounds from the grill, spread with some goat cheese, top with the bruschetta mixture, and serve.

# WHITE CLAM FLATBREAD

White clam pizza originated in New Haven, Connecticut, at Frank Pepe Pizzeria (and if it didn't, go yell at someone other than me). And if Frank hadn't created it, this recipe would probably not be here—cuz, honestly, a clam pizza doesn't sound all that good. But just like the San Diego Fish Taco, which I think also sounds bad—it's quite the contrary and delicious. And, yes, they probably use fresh clams in New Haven, but this little number, with canned, is an easy and mighty fine stand-in.

**MAKES TWO 4-BY-13-INCH FLATBREADS**

⅓ cup sour cream

3 large garlic cloves, minced finely

1 tablespoon olive oil

2 flatbreads, roughly 4 by 13 inches

1 cup shredded mozzarella

Three 6.5-ounce cans chopped white clams, drained

½ cup shredded Parmesan

1 teaspoon red pepper flakes

½ teaspoon kosher salt, or to taste

½ teaspoon coarsely ground black pepper, or to taste

2 tablespoons chopped fresh parsley

1. Preheat a grill to medium-high. Clean and oil the grill grates, and set up for two-zone cooking.

2. Put the sour cream, garlic, and oil in a small bowl and mix well to combine. Spread evenly over the flatbreads.

3. Top with the mozzarella, the drained clams, and finally, the Parmesan.

4. Sprinkle with the red pepper flakes, season to taste with salt and black pepper, and put on the indirect side of the grill. Close the lid.

5. Because the flatbread is parcooked, we're really only waiting for the cheese to melt and get crispier (and by "we," I mean you). But you'll need to rotate the breads every couple of minutes so they cook evenly.

6. When done, maybe 15 to 20 minutes, remove, top with the parsley, cut, and serve.

# CORN, RED ONION & GOAT CHEESE QUESADILLA

There's something about the tanginess of goat cheese that I really love—which maybe not everyone does, but that makes me sad. And when combined with the grilled corn and red onion, it really shines. But if it's not in your wheelhouse, feel free to swap it out for another cheese (but you really should try it!).

**MAKES TWO 8-INCH QUESADILLAS**

2 tablespoons neutral oil

1 ear corn, husked

Two ½-inch-thick slices red onion

8 ounces goat cheese crumbles

½ teaspoon smoked paprika

½ teaspoon red pepper flakes

Kosher salt & coarsely ground black pepper

Four 8-inch tortillas

1. Preheat a grill to medium-high. Clean and oil the grill grates, and set up for two-zone cooking. Close the lid.

2. Lightly brush the corn and red onion with oil and place on the grill. Cook until well marked on both sides: the onion should take about 7 minutes; the corn, about 25.

3. Remove from the grill, and when cool enough to handle, cut the kernels off the corn, dice the onion, and put both into a bowl with the goat cheese, paprika, red pepper flakes, and salt and black pepper to taste. Mix well.

4. Lower the grill heat to medium.

5. Cover each of two tortillas with half of the mixture, then top with other tortillas and press down.

6. Lightly oil the tops of each, then carefully invert onto the grill so the oil side is down.

7. Cook for 2 minutes, or until beginning to get grill marks, then turn 90 degrees and grill until a second set of marks are there. Now, flip over and do same to other side.

8. Cut into wedges and serve.

# KOKODA—FIJIAN CEVICHE

When it comes to summertime grilling (or any grilling, for that matter), a fresh, cool, light appetizer is always welcome. And I've always been a ceviche fan for all those reasons. But this Fijian version with the addition of coconut milk is well, just kinda next level.

**SERVES 4 TO 6**

1 pound mahimahi or red
   snapper fillet, skinned

Juice of about 5 lemons
   and 5 limes

½ small red onion, diced small

3 red Holland chiles,
   finely chopped

2 small tomatoes, chopped small

5 green onions, chopped finely

2 tablespoons chopped
   fresh cilantro

2 cups coconut milk

Kosher salt and coarsely
   ground black pepper

Coconut shell, for serving

Lime wedges, for serving

1. Cut the fish into ½-inch dice and put in a bowl with the lemon and lime juice. Mix well, cover, and let marinate for a couple hours; the fish will turn white when it's ready.

2. Drain the fish and add the red onion, chiles, tomatoes, green onions, cilantro, coconut milk, and salt and black pepper to taste. Mix well and refrigerate.

3. Serve in a coconut shell, with lime wedges.

# VEGGIES

I know grilling and smoking generally mean proteins: beef, chicken, beef, pork, beef—you get the idea. But listen up, cuz your doctor called and asked me to throw in a little healthy love for you. So, I did, and I think you'll like them. The Charred Parmesan Hearts of Palm, or the Grilled Cabbage (don't you dare laugh till you make it, cuz it's so good), added as a side to almost any protein in this book, will be a thing of beauty.

# SOY THYME ONIONS

Daaaaamn. Though you could squish these flat after cooking to use in a burger, that's not really what I have in mind. I like them on the side of a plate, beside a steak or some chicken. A bite of steak, a bite of an onion, a look of happiness.

**MAKES 8 QUARTERS, WHICH SHOULD BE GOOD FOR 4 PEOPLE**

2 large yellow onions
Neutral oil
SPG (page 20)
⅓ cup thick soy (store-bought, or see recipe that follows), or regular soy sauce
Fresh thyme leaves for garnish

1. Preheat a grill to medium-high. Clean and oil the grill grates, and set up for two-zone cooking.
2. Peel the onions. Quarter them but keep the root intact to hold them together; you can take a small slice off the end to clean it up, though.
3. Lightly brush oil on the cut sides of the onions, season with a little SPG, and place cut side down on the direct side of the grill.
4. Grill each cut side for 3 or 4 minutes, or until you start to get char marks.
5. Then, move the onions to the indirect side, baste with the soy, and leave for about 15 minutes for the soy to caramelize a bit and the onions to soften.
6. Remove from the grill, sprinkle with the thyme, and serve.

## THICK SOY

I must admit I'm a huge fan of thick soy (aka soy paste) which, as the name implies, is thicker than regular soy, but also a little sweeter. It's great in stir-fry recipes when you want soy sauce flavor but not the added liquid. Thick soy is easily available at any Asian market and, for sure, online. But here's an easy recipe if you want to make it.

**MAKES ABOUT ½ CUP**

½ cup soy sauce
2 tablespoons light brown sugar

1. Put the soy sauce and brown sugar in a small pot and, while stirring, quickly bring to a boil.
2. As soon as it does and you know the sugar has dissolved, remove from the heat, let cool, and use.

# CHARRED PARMESAN HEARTS OF PALM

Hearts of palm are exactly what you'd think they are: the inner core of (certain) palm trees. If an asparagus stalk and an artichoke had a baby, this is what it might taste like. Sliced and added to salads, they're a no-brainer, and if you haven't used them pick up a can or two. But grilled, when they get beautifully charred, is where they really shine.

**MAKES ABOUT 15 HEARTS**

Two 14-ounce cans hearts of palm, drained, then dried with paper towels

⅓ cup Italian Dressing (page 32)

¼ cup shredded Parmesan

1. Preheat a grill to medium-high. Clean and oil the grill grates.

2. Brush the hearts with a light coating of the dressing.

3. Place the hearts on the grill.

4. Grill, brushing a couple of times with the dressing and turning often, until nicely charred.

5. Remove from the grill, add one last brush of the dressing, sprinkle with the Parm, and serve.

# ITALIAN ELOTE

Regular elote is essentially Mexican street corn: grilled, brushed with mayo, sprinkled with chili powder, and topped with cheese—and it's *muy bien*. But when you change it up and brush it with pesto, it becomes *qualcosa di speciale*—something special.

**MAKES 4 EARS**

4 ears corn, husked, silk removed

Olive oil

Cooking spray for grill

½ cup Basil Pesto (page 27; or store-bought—I won't be mad)

1 teaspoon kosher salt

¼ cup grated or finely shredded fresh Parmesan

1. Preheat a grill to medium-high. Clean the grill grates.

2. Wrap each ear of corn in plastic wrap and microwave on HIGH for 5 minutes. Remove the wrap. Note: You can skip the microwave step, but if you do, increase the grill time to about 25 minutes.

3. Lightly oil each ear of corn. Spray your grill with cooking spray and place the corn on the grill.

4. Cook, turning occasionally, until about 75 percent of the kernels have blackened somewhat, about 10 minutes.

5. Brush the ears well with pesto, and continue to grill another for a couple of minutes to let the pesto "burn" in a bit.

6. Remove from the grill, give one more brushing of pesto, season to taste with salt, and serve garnished with a good sprinkling of Parmesan.

# JILL'S GRILLED HALLOUMI SALAD

Halloumi is a semihard cheese that lands somewhere between feta and mozzarella on the taste scale. But the cool part is that it takes a lot to get it to melt, and that means we can grill it. And I've named this after my assistant Jill, who worked tirelessly every day we shot these photos. She's always happy, superefficient, and quick. But maybe too quick the day we shot this recipe. Because the halloumi slices were all perfectly grilled, just waiting for me to build the salad and Lucas to take the pic when Jill threw them away, thinking they had been sitting out too long. We're still laughing about it.

**SERVES 4**

4 cups mixed greens

1 medium English cucumber, peeled and diced

2 vine-ripened tomatoes, diced

½ cup pitted Kalamata olives, halved

½ cup red onion, diced

Kosher salt and freshly ground black pepper

Italian Dressing (page 32)

One 8-ounce block halloumi, drained of brine, then dried well on paper towels

Chopped fresh parsley for garnish

1. Preheat a grill to medium-high. Clean and oil the grill grates.

2. Combine the greens, cucumber, tomatoes, olives, and red onion in a large bowl and toss to mix. Season with salt and pepper.

3. Cut the halloumi into roughly ½-inch-thick slices, brush with a little of the dressing, and place directly on the grill.

4. Cook until a beautifully golden color starts to develop, anywhere from 3 to 5 minutes, then turn the slices over and repeat.

5. While the slices cook, dress the salad to your liking, and serve topped with the warm, grilled halloumi and garnished with parsley.

# GRILLED EGGPLANT PARM

Traditionally, for an eggplant parm, the eggplant is breaded and then deep-fried, but we're not doing that. We're going natural and all delicious. It's crispy, it's melty, it has huge flavor from the pesto, and I wanna make one just thinking about it . . .

**SERVES 4**

1 large globe eggplant

2 or 3 large tomatoes

Olive oil

Kosher salt and coarsely ground black pepper

4 slices mozzarella

4 crusty Italian-type rolls, sliced lengthwise, leaving a hinge

⅓ cup Basil Pesto (page 27)

⅓ cup shredded Parmesan

1. Preheat a grill to medium-high. Clean and oil the grill grates.

2. Slice the eggplant and tomatoes into eight ¼-inch rounds, then brush lightly with oil and season with salt and pepper.

3. Grill the eggplant and tomato slices until softened and marked with grill lines on both sides.

4. Remove the tomatoes when done, but when you flip the eggplant, slightly overlap the slices in pairs and top with the mozzarella.

5. Brush the cut sides of the rolls with oil, and add, face down, to the grill.

6. When the cheese is melted, remove the eggplant slices from the grill and build: bottom of roll, a layer of pesto, the eggplant with cheese, the tomatoes, and some shredded Parmesan and the top of the roll.

# TWICE-SMOKED SWEET POTATOES

Ah, yes, everyone loves a baked potato. But for me, less is more and those loaded, fridge-clearing, everything-but-the-kitchen sink stuffed ones miss the mark—sorry if this offends. These are much simpler, and because of that, make the perfect side to almost anything.

**MAKES 4 POTATOES**

4 sweet potatoes

Olive oil

Kosher salt

1 large yellow onion

Coarsely ground black pepper

1 garlic head

¼ cup sour cream

1¼ cups shredded smoked Gouda

1 tablespoon Sweet Hot Rub (page 22)

Garlic White Sauce (page 30) for drizzling

2 tablespoons minced chives for garnish

1. Preheat a smoker to 375°F, or read below for grill directions.

2. Scrub the sweet potatoes under cold water, dry well, and poke all over with a fork.

3. Brush them lightly with oil, season with salt, and place on the smoker.

4. Peel the onion, slice in half across the middle, oil lightly on both sides, season with salt and pepper, and add to the smoker.

5. Cut off and discard about ½ inch from the top of the garlic head (the pointy end), put on an 8-inch square of foil, drizzle with a little oil, seal up, then add to the smoker.

6. When the potatoes are soft, in about an hour, remove from the smoker along with the onion and garlic.

7. Slice about one-third off the top of the potatoes, carefully scoop out the inside (I chose not to call it "flesh," which I find so odd)—try to leave about a ¼-inch-thick shell of potato all around—and put the scooped-out potato into a bowl.

8. Finely chop the onion and add to the bowl.

9. Squeeze the garlic out of its skin and also add to the bowl, along with the sour cream, a cup of the Gouda, and the rub. Mash everything well.

10. Season to taste with more salt and pepper, then carefully stuff the filling back into the potatoes, top with the remaining Gouda, and put back into the smoker until melted, about 15 minutes.

11. Serve drizzled with garlic white sauce and topped with chives.

## Grill Method

1. Preheat a grill to high. Clean and oil the grill grates, and set up for two-zone cooking.

2. After oiling and seasoning the sweet potatoes, put them directly on a baking sheet, along with the oiled and seasoned onion and foil-wrapped garlic.

3. After about an hour, proceed as instructed above when the potatoes come off the smoker.

# GRILLED CABBAGE

I'm a fan of cabbage . . . in a soup, a salad, used like that. So, I was pretty sure I was going to like it grilled before I had it the first time. What I didn't know was that I was going to *love* it. And it's all about the simplicity. Oil, salt, and pepper, and that's kind of it. But if you want to go crazy and throw some paprika or chili powder or even drizzle some of the Garlic White Sauce (page 30) on it, go nuts. Because the only thing that really matters is what happens when it gets charred on the grill—cuz it's a whole 'nother animal.

**MAKES 6 SERVINGS**

1 medium head (1.5 to 2 pounds) green cabbage—ohh what the hell . . . make it a red cabbage, if you want

Olive oil

SPG (page 20)

Garlic White Sauce (page 30) for drizzling

1. Preheat a grill to medium-high. Clean and oil the grill grates.

2. Remove any crappy-looking outer leaves from the cabbage, and cut into six wedges, maintaining the core, because that'll hold the wedges together.

3. Brush lightly with oil and season with the SPG.

4. Place cut side down on the grill, and leave for about 4 minutes with no touching, until good char marks appear. Then, flip to the other cut side and repeat.

5. When it's done, it's done, and you have yourself one fine veggie side that will literally go with anything.

6. Especially with a drizzle of the garlic white sauce.

# CHICKEN AND ONE DUCK

Sounds like the beginning of a joke doesn't it: "A chicken and a duck walk into a bar . . ."

But it ain't no joke, cuz a grill and a smoker love chicken and, yes, duck, too. And, not to belabor the point, it's about the charring and the smoke that make it so good.

# You Need To Do These 2 Things

## DRY BRINING

A quick word first: The most important thing you can do to achieve white meat greatness would be to brine before cooking. Brining will make your poultry more tender, more juicy, and definitely more flavorful. You've likely seen it done with a salt-sugar-water solution—and that's simply a pain in the ass. Dry brining gets you to the same place—with no pain.

Using a ratio of approximately 1 tablespoon of kosher salt for about every 3 pounds of chicken, pork, etc. (not table salt, because it'll make it too salty; and not sea salt, because it's more expensive and unnecessary), season both sides of your protein with the salt.

Transfer to a rack set on top of a baking sheet and put in the fridge, uncovered, for 24 hours before cooking.

## SPATCHCOCKING

When it comes to whole chickens or turkeys, the next best thing you can do is to spatchcock them before cooking. This just means you remove the backbone, which lets them lie flat so they cook more evenly and faster.

Put the chicken or turkey breast side down on some paper towels on your counter. The backbone on a chicken is where yours is, and should be obvious. Using good, and by "good" I mean strong, kitchen shears, cut along each side of the backbone; remove and save it for stock or broth. BTW, do you know the difference? Good, cuz no one really does. Okay, technically stock is made from bones; and broth, from meat and vegetables—but they're often used interchangeably, and that's okay.

Now, gently flip the chicken over so it's skin side up, find the center of the breast plate and, using your hands (one on top of the other like you're about to give chest compressions), push down until you hear or feel a crack, or both. Congratulations, you've just successfully spatchcocked, which will make everything better. Seriously, this is a great way to cook poultry, but one question: where the hell did the name come from?

HOW TO SPATCHCOCK

# WINGS 3 WAYS

I think almost everyone loves chicken wings (except for my wife, Kelly, who, if I haven't already said, is my polar food opposite. Not in every case, but in many—and especially when it comes to wings. She won't get near them. But I digress . . . ). Most people like them so much, here are three different recipes.

## SALT, PEPPER & GARLIC–SMOKED

These might've been some of the first wings I ever made, and they're still a favorite today. Is there anything that doesn't benefit from garlic butter?

**MAKES 3 POUNDS, ABOUT 15 WINGS**

1 tablespoon kosher salt

1 tablespoon coarsely ground black pepper

3 pounds wings

2 tablespoons neutral oil

2 tablespoons butter

2 garlic cloves, minced

1. Preheat a smoker to 375°F. No smoker? See below . . .
2. Combine the salt and pepper in a small bowl and mix well.
3. Put the wings in a large bowl with 1 tablespoon of the oil, mix well, then add the salt and pepper mixture and toss to coat. If you have a wire rack, I'd put the wings on that just to make your life easier.
4. Put in the smoker and cook until the internal temperature hits 175°F to 180°F, which should be somewhere around 45 to 60 minutes.
5. When almost done, melt the butter with the garlic in a small saucepan over medium-low heat and cook just until the garlic becomes fragrant. Remove from the heat and set aside.
6. When the wings hit 175°F+, remove from the smoker, put them in a large bowl, toss with some of the garlic butter, and serve.

If you don't have a smoker:

1. Heat a grill to medium-high. Clean and oil the grates, and set up for two-zone cooking.
2. When ready to cook, put the wings on the hot side to give them some good color, then move them to the indirect-heat side and continue to cook, turning often, until approximately 175°F to 180°F.
3. Continue as instructed above when you remove them.

(CONTINUES)

# HULI HULI—CHARCOAL GRILLED

Classic old-school Hawaii, bruddah. We made this when we were shooting the LiVECAST in Kauai, and we all went crazy for them. If you don't know, the LiVECAST was our beginning on YouTube. It was a live combo talk/cooking show—and no one watched, even me. BTW, these are incredible over charcoal, but feel free to grill them on anything, cuz they'll still be good.

**MAKES 3 POUNDS, ABOUT 15 WINGS**

½ cup light brown sugar

½ cup soy sauce

¼ cup ketchup

2 tablespoons Worcestershire sauce

1 teaspoon sesame oil

1 tablespoon sriracha

3 pounds chicken wings

Greens onions for garnish

Sesame seeds for garnish

1. Combine the brown sugar, soy sauce, ketchup, Worcestershire, sesame oil, and sriracha in a small bowl; mix well. This is your marinade.

2. Place the wings in a large bowl and add about three-quarters of the marinade to the chicken; reserve the rest for dipping.

3. Make sure chicken is well coasted and refrigerate for up to a couple of hours.

4. When ready to cook, light a chimney of charcoal or briquettes, and when it's mostly covered with gray ash, spread them out under one side of the grill and let heat with the lid off for 5 minutes.

5. Cook the wings on the hot side to give them some good color, then move them to the indirect-heat side and continue to cook, turning often, until approximately 180°F. Discard the mixture that the chicken had marinated in.

6. Serve, topped with some green onions and sesame seeds— and feel free to use the marinade you set aside for a little extra dipping.

(CONTINUES)

SALT, PEPPER & GARLIC-
SMOKED WINGS

HULI HULI-CHARCOAL
GRILLED WINGS

SWEET HOT-SMOKED,
THEN FRIED WINGS

# SWEET HOT—SMOKED, THEN FRIED

Okay, so a bit more work because of the frying, but when we made these for YouTube, we all agreed they were the best wings we'd made to date. And remember—a cast-iron pan on your gas grill is perfect for outdoor frying.

**MAKE 3 POUNDS, ABOUT 15 WINGS**

3 pounds chicken wings
Neutral oil
Sweet Hot Rub (page 22)

1. Preheat a smoker to 250°F, or read on for how to grill.
2. Lightly oil the chicken wings, then sprinkle generously with the rub.
3. Place on the smoker and cook until 165°F, then remove from the smoker.
4. Fill a large cast-iron pan with about an inch of oil and heat to 350°F.
5. Cook the wings in batches so you don't overcrowd them, about 2 minutes, flipping over halfway through or until about 180°F.
6. Transfer to a rack, sprinkle with a little more rub, and serve.

No smoker, no problem:

1. Preheat a grill to medium-high. Clean and oil the grill grates, and set up for two-zone cooking.
2. Put the wings on the hot side to give them some good color, then move to the indirect-heat side and continue to cook, turning often, until about 165°F.
3. Then, remove from the grill, and follow the above frying instructions.

# THE HSP—HALAL SNACK PACK

This export comes all the way from Australia and might just be one of the best reasons to go there to visit. Oh, sure, there's amazing natural beauty, the weather is near perfect, and the cities are vibrant and exciting. But the HSP, with its crispy fries, melty cheese, and perfectly cooked chicken with not one, not two, but *three* sauces is something you must have. BTW, down there, the meat (usually lamb or chicken) is normally cooked in one of those stand-up rotisserie *doner* things. But since most of us don't have one, getting a good char on the chicken will not just be delicious, but also important. One note: Halal is the Muslim practice for how an animal is raised, fed, and slaughtered; it's similar to kosher. So, technically, this is halal in name only, unless you get yourself some halal chicken. But, either way, you'll be happy you made it.

**SERVES 4 OR 5**

1½ pounds boneless, skinless chicken thighs

3 tablespoons olive oil

1 tablespoon dried oregano

1 tablespoon ground cumin

1 tablespoon ground coriander

1 tablespoon garlic powder

Juice of ½ lemon

Good pinch each of kosher salt and coarsely ground black pepper

Cooking spray for grill

25 ounces fresh hot fries

Chicken Salt (recipe follows; optional)

8 ounces shredded mozzarella

Sweet & Smoky BBQ Sauce (page 23)

Sriracha

Garlic White Sauce (page 30)

1. Put the chicken in a medium bowl and add the oil, oregano, cumin, coriander, garlic powder, lemon juice, salt, and pepper. Mix well, then cover the bowl and refrigerate for a couple of hours up to overnight.

2. Remove the chicken from the fridge 30 minutes before cooking.

3. Heat a grill to high, clean and oil the grill grates, then put on the chicken—your goal is to cook it hot and fast, getting great grill marks yet still keeping it moist and tender. Pull it off at 160°F, then chop into bite-size pieces, and keep warm under foil until you use it.

4. When you're ready to serve, put a pile of fries in a bowl, sprinkle generously with chicken salt (if using), top with a nice layer of mozzarella, then a nice layer of the chicken, then drizzle with equal parts of the BBQ sauce, sriracha, and garlic white sauce.

5. Eat and say, "Australia—cheers to you, mate!"

## CHICKEN SALT

2 tablespoons kosher salt

3 tablespoons chicken bouillon powder

1. Combine the salt and bouillon powder in a small bowl and mix well. Store in a sealed container.

2. Use on anything you want—fries, chicken, avo toast, etc.—for a bit of a savory blast.

# THE CHICKEN WE MAKE ALL THE TIME

There are a handful of dinners that are firmly on repeat in our house, and this is way at the top. Prep it, throw it in the fridge, and cook it the next day. You'll thank me. And, of course, you can cook it and eat it with a knife and fork—but when you throw it in a pita with the Garlic White Sauce (page 30) like the picture, you're in for a delicious ride.

**SERVES 4**

¾ cup olive oil

2 tablespoons Asian fish sauce*

1 tablespoon soy sauce

1 tablespoon Dijon mustard

2 large garlic cloves, minced

2 teaspoons dried thyme

2 teaspoons dried rosemary

½ teaspoon kosher salt

½ teaspoon freshly ground black pepper

Juice of 2 lemons

2 chicken breasts

For serving: pita, diced tomatoes, and cucumber

Garlic White Sauce (page 30)

1. Combine the oil, fish sauce, soy sauce, Dijon, garlic, thyme, rosemary, salt, pepper, and lemon juice in a pint-size measuring cup or deli container and mix or shake well to combine. Set aside.

2. Flatten the chicken breasts to about an even ½-inch thickness, then put into a resealable plastic bag.

3. Add about three-quarters of the marinade, and mush around to ensure chicken is well covered. Then, seal the bag and refrigerate for a couple of hours to overnight. Reserve the remaining marinade for brushing after grilling.

4. Remove from the fridge at least 30 minutes before cooking.

5. Heat a grill to high, clean and oil the grill grates, then cook the chicken, turning often, until you get good grill marks on both sides (which you want, BTW) and the chicken hits approximately 160°F.

6. Remove from the grill, brush with the reserved marinade, slice, and serve in a warm pita, with some tomatoes, cucumbers, and the garlic white sauce over the top.

*If you don't have fish sauce, you could easily swap it out for the same amount of anchovy paste, or Worcestershire. But here's the thing—fish sauce is really good, and like anchovy paste, delivers a wonderful umami (savory) punch. And despite the name, it will not turn your food to a fishy, gross mess—it will just add a much deeper, more beautiful flavor.

# JERKED CHICKEN LEGS

The first time I made this, Kelly almost came out of her shoes. It's spicy, it's sweet, and it's deeply flavored. Of course, you can use any chicken part you want, but since legs are typically eaten with your hands, things get a bit messier, and that means this fantastic sauce all over—and that's a good thing. I told Kelly I was writing out this recipe, and she instantly requested it for dinner tonight. Instantly.

**SERVES 4 TO 5**

10 chicken legs, or thighs
  (or 5 breasts, if you must)
Jerk Sauce (page 26)

1. Place the chicken legs in a resealable plastic bag or shallow dish and add the jerk sauce (reserving about one-quarter of the sauce for later). Be sure all the chicken is well coated, seal, and refrigerate for at least a couple of hours or up to overnight.

2. Remove from the fridge about 30 minutes prior to cooking. If smoking instead of grilling, see the smoker option that follows.

3. When ready to grill, set up for two-zone cooking—one side is set to medium-high and the other to low.

4. Clean and oil the grill grates, then add the chicken to the hot side. Discard the mixture it had marinated in.

5. Cook, turning often, until the chicken is charred lightly in spots but looking beautiful, about 10 minutes.

6. Now, move chicken to the low-heat side and brush with the reserved jerk sauce.

7. Grill, covered, turning often, for another 10 to 15 minutes, until the chicken is 175° to 180°F.

Smoker Option:

1. Preheat a smoker to 275°F.

2. Remove the legs from the jerk sauce, discarding the mixture it had marinated in, place on a smoker rack, and smoke for about 1½ hours, or until 175° to 180°F, brushing with the reserved marinade a couple of times throughout.

*Of course the sauce is great on this, but think of it for other things, such as pork, beef, and shrimp—holy crap!

# BOB'S KOREAN FIRE CHICKEN

I learned to cook chicken from my brother-in-law Bob. In Toronto. On his deck. In his backyard. In winter. In a shit ton of snow. But that was Bob, because when it came to grilling, he was always all in. No one was more committed, dedicated, or willing to share his knowledge—nope, make that share his "craft," because he really knew what the hell he was doing. And it didn't matter what the weather was, because the grill still worked if you were willing to work it. We don't have Bob anymore, but my memories of his patient teaching that freezing, snowy effing day on his back deck are as clear as anything and will never fade. He taught me how to cook chicken, but the addition of the spicy Korean component is my shout-out to his love of fiery food. The man loved his shit hot.

**MAKES 6 THIGHS**

KOREAN FIRE SAUCE*
½ cup gochujang**
¼ cup hot honey
¼ cup soy sauce
2 tablespoons light brown sugar
1 tablespoon rice vinegar
1 tablespoon smoked paprika
1 tablespoon chipotle chile powder
1 teaspoon cayenne pepper
2 tablespoons garlic paste
1 tablespoon ginger paste
2 teaspoons sesame oil
2 teaspoons kosher salt
3 tablespoons water

BOB'S CHICKEN
6 bone-in, skin-on chicken thighs
Sesame seeds and diced
  green onions for garnish

**Gochujang is Korean red pepper paste, and available from most supermarkets or online. I also suggest you double the sauce next time, cuz it'll keep for a couple of weeks in your fridge, and then you'll be ready on a moment's notice to make something with it again. BTW, wings love it!

1. Combine sauce ingredients in a bowl and mix well.

2. Make the chicken: Clean and oil the grill grates, and set for two-zone cooking, with the hot side preheated to medium-high.

3. Brush the skin side of the thighs with the sauce, then place skin side down on the hot side of the grill.

4. Bob would tell you we want good char marks on this side, but they won't take long—so check after 2 minutes, and if they are looking good, give them a 45-degree turn and cook for another couple of minutes—and this is the time to brush the top side with the sauce.

5. When the second set of marks looks good, flip the thighs—and repeat on the bottom side the same way. When the bottom is good, move everything over to the indirect side.

6. Now, this is the part you want a cocktail, beer, soda, something in your hand, as you're not going anywhere. Because even though you're cooking the thighs on the less hot side, there's still some maneuvering to do. You want them all exposed to the heat in as even a manner as possible—and that might mean a little jockeying for position. The thicker thighs should spend more time closer to the hot side, but you can't ignore the smaller ones. You're also flipping them over and then back again, to guarantee even cooking throughout. After about 15 minutes, feel free to give 'em another baste—and this is also the time to start checking with your thermometer.

7. We're looking for 175°F, and when you get there, remove the thighs from the grill and tent them loosely with foil. Let rest for 10 minutes before eating.

8. If you like this chicken, and I know you will, thank Bob. He loved chicken, but he also loved attention.

# TEQUILA LIME CHICKEN TACOS

There's no way anything with tequila, lime, and chicken is going to be bad. And while these become tacos, I encourage you to think outside the tortilla for what else you could use the cooked chicken for. A burrito would be a no-brainer, but how about with chilaquiles, or cut up on top of Mexican rice for a bowl, or in a salad, or on a pizza? You're only limited by your you-know-what.

**MAKES ABOUT TEN
5-INCH TACOS**

Juice of 4 limes

Juice of 1 orange

¼ cup neutral oil

4 garlic cloves

1½ teaspoons chipotle chile powder

1½ teaspoons dried oregano

1½ teaspoons smoked paprika

A big fat pinch each of kosher salt and freshly ground black pepper

¼ cup soy sauce

3 tablespoons chopped fresh cilantro, plus more for serving

½ cup tequila

1½ to 2 pounds boneless, skinless chicken thighs

Corn or flour tortillas

Shredded green cabbage for serving

Avocado Crema (recipe follows)

1. Combine the citrus juices, oil, garlic, chipotle chile powder, oregano, paprika, salt, black pepper, soy sauce, cilantro, and tequila in a medium bowl and mix well. Transfer to a sealable container, add the chicken, and refrigerate for at least a couple of hours up to overnight.

2. Remove the chicken from the fridge 30 minutes before cooking.

3. Preheat a grill to high. Clean and oil the grill grates.

4. Place the chicken on the grill and cook, turning often, until really good char marks appear and the chicken is cooked through—we're looking for about 175°F—then remove from the grill and let rest, loosely covered with foil, for about 5 minutes.

5. Chop the chicken into smaller, bite-size pieces.

6. Build: Heat a tortilla on the grill until grill marks appear, then add some cabbage, some chicken, and some crema, and top with a bit more cilantro.

7. Eat and repeat.

## AVOCADO CREMA

**MAKES ABOUT 1 CUP**

1 ripe avocado, peeled and pitted

¼ cup nonfat plain Greek yogurt

¼ cup chopped fresh cilantro

2 tablespoons milk, perhaps more depending on the size of your avo

1 large garlic clove, minced

Zest and juice of 1 lime

Kosher salt and coarsely ground black pepper

Put everything, including salt and pepper to taste, into a blender or food processor, and blend until it's where you want it, thickness-wise. Add more milk to make it slightly thinner, if you like.

# YOGURT-MARINATED CHICKEN WITH CURRY

Once again, we see how the addition of a couple of simple ingredients can make a huge change to a dish. In this case, it's the curry and turmeric that take this in a whole new direction.

**SERVES 4**

8 ounces plain nonfat Greek yogurt—you could use regular yogurt, but the nonfat gives it extra tang

Zest and juice of 1 lemon

2 garlic cloves, crushed

2 tablespoons neutral oil

1 tablespoon sriracha

⅓ cup chopped fresh cilantro, plus 2 tablespoons for garnish

1 teaspoon kosher salt

2 teaspoons ground cumin

2 teaspoons curry powder

2 teaspoons turmeric (no turmeric? no prob; just double up on the curry powder)

4 chicken leg quarters

Coconut Rice for serving (recipe follows)

1. Combine everything, except the chicken and the coconut rice, in a large bowl and whisk well. This is your sauce.

2. Set aside about ⅓ cup of the sauce, and add the chicken to the rest. Make sure it's well coated, cover, and refrigerate for a couple of hours up to overnight.

3. Remove the chicken from fridge about 30 minutes before cooking.

4. Preheat a grill to medium-high. Clean and oil the grill grates, and set up for two-zone cooking.

5. Start by cooking the chicken skin side down on the hot side a couple of minutes, then flip them over and repeat. Discard the mixture the chicken had marinated in.

6. Move the leg quarters to the indirect side and continue to cook, brushing occasionally with the reserved sauce, until done at approximately 175°F.

7. Serve with the coconut rice, garnished with the remaining cilantro.

## COCONUT RICE

This rice is nice and light with just the right amount of coconut. It's perfect for so many things, but pairs really well with the chicken. Oh, the little flecks you see are just rice that has started to burn a bit on the bottom—something you definitely want. Extra taste, texture, and just look at how beautiful it makes it.

**MAKES ABOUT 3 CUPS**

1 cup uncooked jasmine or basmati rice

One 13.5-ounce can coconut milk

½ cup water

1 teaspoon sugar

½ teaspoon kosher salt

1. Rinse the rice well until the water runs clear, then put into a medium pot with the coconut milk, water, sugar, and salt.

2. Bring to a boil, then cover and lower the heat to a simmer. Cook until all the liquid has been absorbed, 10 to 12 minutes.

3. Remove from the heat and let the rice sit, covered, for 5 to 10 minutes before fluffing and serving.

# SMOKED WHOLE DUCK

You know the old "tastes like chicken" adage? Well, it's funny that the one thing you would def think tasted like chicken—doesn't. I also think it's funny how many people don't like duck—or say they don't. I think it's less about taste and more about, well, that it's a duck. So, let's change that right now, and let this be your duck coming-out party. And if you don't already have Chinese five-spice powder, it's certainly worth getting for this and making the Char Siu—Chinese BBQ Pork (page 118).

**MAKES 1 DUCK**

1 whole duck (4 to 5 pounds)

2 tablespoons Chinese five-spice powder

2 tablespoon kosher salt (optional)

1 tablespoon sugar

2 teaspoons garlic powder

¼ cup sesame oil

⅓ cup pure maple syrup

½ cup apricot jam

1. If you're so inclined (and you should be), dry brine the duck first for 24 hours (see page 74 for how to do this).

2. Remove the duck from the fridge 30 minutes before cooking.

3. Combine the five-spice powder, salt (only if you haven't dry brined), sugar, and garlic powder in a small bowl and mix well.

4. Brush the duck all over with sesame oil and season with the five-spice mixture.

5. Preheat a smoker to 275°F. (If you don't have a smoker, see the instructions that follow.) Hang the duck in the barrel or lay on the smoker rack, and close the lid.

6. After about an hour of cooking, combine the maple syrup and jam in a small pan over low heat to let melt together, then brush on the duck.

7. Baste every 20 minutes or so until you get an internal temperature of 160°F.

8. Remove from the smoker and let rest for 20 minutes before carving.

No Smoker?

Just set your oven to 275°F, put your duck on a rack on a baking sheet, and do everything else the same.

# SEAFOOD

A lot of people seem to stay away from cooking seafood outdoors, which leaves me scratching my head. Is it because they think it's complicated? Is it because they believe the outdoors was made for hearty things, like whole roasts and pork butts? Or maybe, it's because many people fall into a rut: "You know Dan; he only cooks two thing out there . . . his steaks and his chops." Well, Dan is being a dick, and needs to change.

I always say, "Don't eat the same thing all the time," and this chapter (like the whole book) echoes that thinking. And there's more than just fish in here. We have fun with lotsa stuff from the sea.

# First, and It Should Be Obvious . . .

Whatever fish you choose should be as fresh as possible. Fish, while certainly can be frozen, is not like beef or poultry. A frozen rib eye comes back to life from frozen and cooks beautifully—this is not exactly true of salmon or snapper, for example. Shrimp and scallops are an exception, but most fish lose quality after defrosting. So, how do you know it's as fresh as the sign says? This would be a good time to get to know a fishmonger—because that's all they do. Yes, of course, fish is sold at a supermarket, and the people behind the counter might be great, but they also may have just come from the bakery department the day before and actually know nothing.

So, I turned to my dear friend in San Diego, Tommy Gomes—fishmonger extraordinaire. He sells fish at his TunaVille Market, has a TV show called *The Fishmonger*, and knows more about fish than anyone I know—maybe even the fish themselves. And while he's a cantankerous bastard who could likely offend your grandmother without saying anything, he really knows his shit. Here's his advice on picking fish and seafood:

- Look for the fish to have clear eyes; they should never be cloudy.
- When you press on the skin, it should bounce back and not leave a finger dent.
- And this one might be counterintuitive, but your fish shouldn't smell like fish, but rather like salt or the sea.

And lastly, the old pain in the ass dropped a final piece of his fishmonger wisdom. He said to remember that *"good fish isn't cheap, and cheap fish isn't good."*

Thank you, Thomas; true words.

With that said, let's head into the chapter with an open mind, and a pledge to try the recipes. You don't want to be a dick like Dan.

TUNA BEING GRILLED FOR THE GRILLED TUNA SALAD

# HERBED SALMON

This is a great way to start this chapter because it's not just delicious, but also simple and you can't mess it up. And not only is salmon one of the greatest foods to cook outside, but this is also one of the easiest ways to make it. And I know 250°F sounds low, but the end result is the most herbaceous, perfectly cooked, tender, and medium rare salmon you may ever have. And if "medium-rare" salmon discourages you, remember one thing. If people can eat completely raw salmon at a sushi place, you can eat medium-rare salmon in your backyard.

**SERVES 6 TO 8**

1 side of salmon
   (about 3 pounds), skin on

¼ cup Kewpie brand Japanese
   mayonnaise (preferably)
   or regular mayonnaise

1 to 2 tablespoons sriracha

Kosher salt and freshly
   ground black pepper

½ cup fresh dill, finely chopped

½ cup finely diced green onions,
   white & light green parts only

½ cup fresh curly parsley,
   chopped finely

1. Preheat a smoker to 250°F.

2. Put the salmon skin side down on a large piece of parchment paper.

3. Combine the mayo and sriracha in a small bowl, brush a layer on the salmon, then season the salmon well with salt and pepper.

4. Place the dill, green onions, and parsley in a bowl, mix well, then top the salmon with the mixture until you only see green.

5. Smoke for 30 minutes, or until about 125°F, for perfectly tender, medium rare salmon.

# GRILLED TUNA SALAD

This is not the tuna salad you might be thinking, which is a good thing. But cooking it properly is very important, so have a good read through first, because done right, you'll be the star of the street. And BTW, this is so fresh and so healthy—you can and should eat it often.

**SERVES 4**

2 avocados

⅓ English cucumber

1 pound block fresh tuna

1½ teaspoons sesame oil

Cooking spray

1½ tablespoons soy sauce

1 tablespoon rice vinegar

1 teaspoon wasabi paste

1 large garlic clove, minced finely

½ teaspoon ginger paste
    or grated fresh ginger

Juice of ¼ lime
    (about 1½ teaspoons)

Kosher salt

2 green onions, white and light
    green parts only, chopped finely

Furikake* or toasted sesame
    seeds for garnish

*Furikake is a very popular Japanese condiment (made up of seaweed, sesame seeds, herbs, etc.) that's used on everything from seafood to rice and vegetables. My kids grew up with it, and had it on plain steamed white rice as a snack after school. We love it. Just go find some online, cuz sesame seeds on this are good—but the furikake makes it great.

1. Peel and pit the avocados and dice as neatly as you can into ½-inch pieces. Put into a bowl.

2. Do the same with the half cucumber and put into the same bowl.

3. Preheat a grill to high, clean and oil the grill grates, then close the lid.

4. Read this step fully before cooking the tuna: Brush both sides of the tuna with some of the sesame oil—but here's the thing: When the grill is really hot, and only then, spray the grates with cooking spray, then put the tuna down and give it 15 to 20 seconds, then turn it 45 degrees and give it 15 to 20 seconds more, then flip . . . but this time, put it on a freshly sprayed part of the grill the tuna hasn't previously been on (we still want it on a fresh, hot part of the grill). Give it another 15 to 20 seconds, then do a 45-degree turn and give it 15 to 20 seconds more, then, finally, transfer it to a plate to rest. If your grill was hot enough, your tuna will be spectacular.

5. While the salmon cools, make the soy dressing: Combine the remaining sesame oil, soy sauce, rice vinegar, wasabi paste, garlic, ginger, lime juice, and salt to taste in a small bowl and mix well.

6. Cut the now-cooled tuna into ½-inch dice and add it to the avocado mixture, along with the chopped green onion. Add some, not all, of the soy dressing, to your liking. Mix gently to coat, and then plate.

7. Garnish with furikake or sesame seeds (but it really should be furikake).

# WHOLE GRILLED FISH WITH PEPPER SALSA

Cooking any kind of fish on the grill freaks the eff out of many people, and even more so when it comes to a whole fish, to the point where many won't even try it. Well, that ends now, because not only will the mayo we use add flavor and moisture, but it's your secret weapon for making the fish almost nonstick.

## SERVES 4 TO 6

2 whole small fish, such as a snapper, branzino, trout, etc.
1 teaspoon celery salt
Coarsely ground black pepper
1 bunch cilantro
1 lime, sliced thinly
⅓ cup mayonnaise
Kosher salt

PEPPER SALSA
2 tablespoons olive oil
½ green bell pepper, diced finely
½ red bell pepper, diced finely
½ onion—any color, diced
1 jalapeño pepper, diced finely
1 large garlic clove, minced
Juice of 1 lime
Kosher salt and freshly ground black pepper

1. Remove the fish from the refrigerator about 30 minutes before cooking.

2. Dry the fish really well with paper towels, and make three or four diagonal cuts into the flesh (between the head and tail) on each side.

3. Season the cavity of each fish with the celery salt and black pepper, then stuff with five or six sprigs of the cilantro (reserve the rest of the cilantro for the salsa) and three or four lime slices.

4. Close up, brush mayo on both sides of the fish, then season with salt and black pepper.

5. Preheat a grill to medium-high Clean and oil the grill grates.

6. Gently put the fish directly on the grates; alternatively, you could use a fish basket.

7. Now, don't touch the fish and just let it grill until the bottom starts to char, about 5 minutes—you can check by using a spatula to gently left the fish, or even use a carving fork to get in between the grates under the fish. In either case, if it's still sticking, give it another minute. When you can lift it easily from the grill, gently turn onto the other side and cook for about 5 minutes longer, or until an instant-read digital thermometer reads 135°F.

8. While the fish cook, make the salsa: Heat a small nonstick pan over medium-high heat, add about 1 tablespoon of the oil, and when it is just getting ready to smoke, put in the bell peppers, onion, and jalapeño.

9. Stir until just softened, add the garlic, and when fragrant, remove from the heat and transfer a bowl. Add 3 tablespoons of chopped fresh cilantro, the lime juice, and the remaining tablespoon of oil. Mix well and season to taste with salt and black pepper, then set aside.

10. When the fish is done, let rest for 5 minutes, then serve with the salsa.

# CREOLE FISH SANDWICHES WITH SPICY PICKLED MAYO

Pickled mayonnaise and grilled catfish . . . it's like a bit of the South right where you are. Unless you're already there; then, it's like . . . oh, never mind.

**MAKES 4 SANDWICHES**

Four 6-ounce catfish fillets, or any similar white fish, such as flounder or haddock

4 buns (something with a little crisp would be great here)

About 1 cup Goes-with-Anything Coleslaw (page 227)

1 large tomato, sliced

SPICY PICKLED MAYO

¾ cup mayonnaise

2 tablespoons Old Bay seasoning

1 large dill pickle, diced finely (about ¼ cup)

1½ teaspoons Creole-style mustard, or spicy brown mustard will do just fine

½ teaspoon smoked paprika

1 teaspoon prepared horseradish

1. Preheat a grill to medium-high. Clean and oil the grill grates.

2. Brush one side of fish lightly with mayo, season with Old Bay, and put mayo side down on the grill.

3. Cook for 4 to 5 minutes without moving the fish, then brush some mayo onto and season the top. Gently flip over and cook for another 4 to 5 minutes, or until the fish can flake easily with a fork.

4. While it cooks, combine the remaining mayo, pickle, mustard, paprika, and horseradish in a small bowl and mix well.

5. Slice the buns in half and place, face down, on the grill, to toast.

6. To build, spread the pickled mayo on the bun bottom, add some coleslaw, tomato slice(s), the fish, and finally the bun top.

# HALIBUT WITH CAST-IRON TOMATOES

Eat more fish—you hear that all the time—and this will help. Something incredible happens to tomatoes when they hit a hot cast-iron pan and start to char. And when they get added to a beautifully grilled piece of fish, all's right with the world.

**SERVES 4**

Four 6-ounce halibut fillets, or any white fish, really

Kosher salt and coarsely ground black pepper

1 teaspoon smoked paprika

1 teaspoon garlic powder

¼ cup mayonnaise

1 pound teardrop or cherry tomatoes

Olive oil

1 garlic clove, minced

Zest of 1 lemon

⅓ cup sour cream

Chopped fresh parsley for garnish

1. Preheat a grill to medium-high. Clean and oil the grill grates.

2. Put a medium cast-iron pan on the grill to heat.

3. Season both sides of the halibut with salt, pepper, paprika, and garlic powder.

4. Then, brush the top side of the halibut lightly with mayo (which works to help keep the fish essentially nonstick) and put mayo side down directly on the grates. Cook for 5 minutes, then brush the remaining mayo on the side facing up, and turn over.

5. Cook for another 5 minutes, or until the fish is opaque and flakes easily.

6. When you first put the fish on, toss the tomatoes with 1 tablespoon of the oil, season with salt and pepper, and then add to the cast-iron pan.

7. Stir the tomatoes so they begin to char all the way around, and when they've softened after about 5 minutes, add the garlic and stir. When fragrant, remove from the heat, add the lemon juice, and set aside.

8. When the fish is done, serve with some sour cream, the tomatoes, and a little parsley.

# KING CRAB LEGS

Considering the legs come already cooked, this is really less about cooking and more about warming. But warming with flavor from chili butter that results in a big payoff. And, of course, you can cook these on a gas grill, but when they're done over charcoal, something magical happens.

**SERVES 2 TO 3**

8 tablespoons (1 stick) butter
3 garlic cloves, crushed
2 teaspoons chili powder
½ teaspoon kosher salt
½ teaspoon coarsely
   ground black pepper
4 pounds king crab legs

1. Heat a charcoal grill to medium-high—and make sure the grill grates are superclean. Oil the grates.

2. Put the butter, garlic, chili powder, salt, and black pepper in a small pot over low heat to melt; stir well to mix.

3. I like to separate the knuckles from the crab legs, and once done, use kitchen shears to cut about a ¼-inch-wide trench up the inside of each leg.

4. Pull the shell sides back slightly to expose the meat, then use a brush to get the chili butter inside the shell and onto as much of the crabmeat as possible. Give the outside a light coating and brush the butter all the way around the knuckles.

5. Put on the grill and cover (to smoke, see the instructions that follow) and let cook, flipping often, for 10 to 12 minutes total, until nicely warmed through.

6. When done, just remove from the grill and serve with the remaining chili butter.

To smoke them:

Preheat your smoker to 250°F, and after cutting and brushing with the butter, put them on and smoke about 30 minutes, or until heated through.

# MUSSELS WITH GARLIC ANCHOVY BUTTER

This is about as adventuresome as I'll ask you to get in this chapter—which, frankly, isn't much at all. Mussels are delicious, fun to eat, and perfect for sharing—and not difficult to cook. And the anchovy paste just adds an amazing background note, so don't be scared. Just go ahead and use it.

**SERVES 2 TO 4**

3 pounds mussels

2 tablespoons olive oil

4 tablespoons (½ stick) butter

4 red Holland peppers or 3 red jalapeño peppers, diced finely

½ red onion, diced

3 tablespoons minced garlic

1 cup half-and-half

2 teaspoons anchovy paste

1 cup vermouth or white wine

Finely chopped something green for a garnish: fresh chives, green onion, fresh parsley—they're all good

Baguette or any kind of crusty bread for dipping

1. Rinse the mussels under cold water and give a gentle scrubbing to clean—don't forget to pull off the mussel's "beard," the creepy little hairy part sticking out from the straight side of the shell.

2. Make sure all the shells are closed, and if any are open, give them a gentle tap on the counter. If they don't close up, throw them away along with any that are cracked. BTW, one more reason to use a good fishmonger, cuz they'll leave those ones out.

3. Heat a grill to high and put a large, grillproof pan on it; cast iron is ideal, and even a large foil pan will work (but serving out of one is not so pretty).

4. Pour the oil into the pan with the butter, and when hot and the butter melted, add the peppers and red onion and cook until they soften, 3 to 4 minutes, then add the garlic.

5. Meanwhile, put the half-and-half in a bowl and whisk in the anchovy paste, whisking just enough to combine.

6. When the pan mixture is fragrant, add the vermouth and mussels. Stir to coat, cover with a lid, and cook until most of the mussels have opened, 3 to 4 minutes.

7. Remove the lid, lower the heat to low, add anchovy paste mixture, and mix.

8. Bring slowly to a simmer to let thicken slightly—but not too fast, or the half-and-half could separate. Simmer for a couple more minutes, or until all the shells have opened (throw away any that haven't).

9. Garnish with your choice of something green and serve right outta the pan with the crusty bread for dipping.

# GRILLED HOISIN SCALLOPS

I've always said that by simply adding a few Asian condiments to the door of your fridge, you can really change your food world. And this is about as simple as it gets—plus, an easy way to dip your toe into another food culture.

**SERVES 3 OR 4**

12 large sea scallops

Neutral oil

Kosher salt and coarsely ground black pepper

⅓ cup hoisin sauce

1 tablespoon Asian chili sauce

Sesame seeds

1. If using wooden skewers, please soak them in water for at least an hour first.

2. Heat a grill to high. Clean and grill the grill grates.

3. Skewer the scallops and lightly coat with neutral oil, then season with salt and black pepper.

4. Combine the hoisin and chili sauce in a small bowl; mix well, then set aside.

5. Grill the scallops until good grill marks develop, 2 to 3 minutes, flip and brush the sauce mixture on the marked side.

6. Cook until the second side is done, brush both sides well with the sauce mixture, and add a little sprinkle of sesame seeds to serve.

# GARLIC-GINGER LOBSTER TAILS

I love this recipe because you get all the sweet, delicious flavor of lobster, but with none of the guilt from having to plunge a whole one into boiling water. Lobster tails are readily available at most seafood stores or supermarkets—and often have been frozen, which is okay in this case. And, if you see them frozen, and on sale—get a few extra; you won't be sorry.

**MAKES 4 TAILS**

4 tablespoons (½ stick) butter

2 tablespoons sriracha

1 large garlic clove, minced

2 teaspoons minced fresh ginger

1 tablespoon chopped fresh chives, green onion, or fresh parsley—just something green

Juice of ¼ lemon

Four lobster tails, 6 to 7 ounces each (or bigger; it's up to you, Rockefeller)

Small pinch each of kosher salt and freshly ground black pepper

1. Preheat a grill to medium-high. Clean and oil the grill grates.

2. Combine all the ingredients, except the tails, salt, and pepper, in small saucepan over low heat until melted, then remove from the heat and set aside.

3. Lay a lobster tail vertically on the counter with the tail part farthest away from you.

4. Put the point of one side of kitchen shears under the shell but above the meat, and cut up the middle of the shell toward the tail, without cutting through the tail.

5. Using that cut as your guide, take a knife and cut down through the meat without cutting through the bottom shell/plate, whatever it's called.

6. Pull back the sides of the shell like you're opening a book, to expose the meat, and brush with some of the butter mixture.

7. Grill the tails meat side down for approximately 5 minutes, then turn them over and cook for another 3 to 4 minutes, basting often, until done—done is 135°F.

8. Remove from the grill, season with a little pinch each of salt and pepper, and serve with any leftover butter sauce.

# PORK AND VEAL

"Pork, the other white meat" never sounded like a good marketing line to me. Imagine if someone said to you, "Oh, you're that other guy." It just doesn't work. And while veal kind of has a foot in everyone's camp (often compared to beef and chicken), pork has to be feeling sorry for itself. So, let's make up for that shitty advertising line, and start eating more pork. And in keeping with my love of "opf" (other people's food), we'll travel to China, Argentina, Mexico, and the Philippines for inspiration in these pork recipes.

# CHAR SIU–CHINESE BBQ PORK

Anyone who knows me knows of my lifelong love affair with Asian food—all of it. And *char siu* (pronounced like the name Sue) might just be at the top of the pile. This, of course, makes a tremendous appetizer and is insanely delicious chopped up in fried rice. But my favorite way to eat it is in a rice bowl, with vegetables like shiitake mushrooms, green onions, and a perfectly cooked sunny-side-up fried egg. Heaven.

**MAKES 3 POUNDS**

SAUCE*
½ cup soy sauce
¼ cup ketchup
⅓ cup light brown sugar
¼ cup hoisin sauce
4 garlic cloves, minced
⅓ cup honey
¼ cup Shaoxing cooking wine, or everyday dry sherry
1 tablespoon Chinese five-spice powder
½ teaspoon ground white pepper if you have it; if not, freshly ground black is fine

3 pounds boneless pork shoulder, sliced into 2-by-1-inch strips
Chinese hot mustard for serving

*This sauce also *loves* chicken. So feel free to marinate chicken thighs in it, then grill them for a nice change.

1. Make the sauce by putting all the sauce ingredients in a medium bowl and mixing well.

2. Reserve about one-third of the mixture, then put the pork and remaining sauce in a resealable plastic bag, make sure the pork is well coated and refrigerate overnight—and overnight is important. You can shorten the marinating time for a lot of recipes, just not this one please.

3. The next day, remove the pork from the fridge about 30 minutes before cooking, to bring to room temperature.

4. Preheat a grill to medium-high. Clean and oil the grill grates.

5. Put on the pork (discard the sauce it had marinated in) and cook, turning often and basting with the reserved marinade until an instant-read digital thermometer hits 145°F, approximately 20 minutes.

6. Remove from the grill, brush once more with the reserved sauce, slice into ¼-inch pieces, and serve with the hot mustard for dipping.

# CHORIPAN ARGENTINA

*Chori* is chorizo, and *pan* is bread—see where this is going? When grilled fresh chorizo sausage finds its way into a crusty roll with chimichurri, it becomes a legendary Argentinean street food. And since I've already covered chimichurri, this is kind of a no-brainer. And, ideally you're looking for Argentinean or Spanish chorizo, just not Mexican chorizo—not that there's anything wrong with that, but it's a whole different thing.

**MAKES 4 SANDWICHES**

4 links fresh Argentinean or Spanish chorizo sausages

1 or 2 fresh baguettes—this will depend on the length of your chorizo, because you want the bread to fit the sausage

Roughly 1¼ cups chimichurri, green or red (page 29)

1. Preheat a grill to medium-high. Clean and oil the grill grates.

2. Put the chorizo on the grill. If it's fresh, cook for 10 to 15 minutes, turning often. If it's fully cooked, then you're simply heating and charring, and this should take 5 to 7 minutes.

3. Just as the sausage is finishing, cut the baguette into the lengths of the sausage, brush lightly with chimichurri, and grill for a minute or so to crisp up and add grill marks.

4. When the sausage is done, you can either add directly to the bun—or slice lengthwise, leaving a hinge, and throw back on to the grill for another couple of minutes to char up the cut side. Then just add the sausage to the bun, spoon a little more chimi on top, and serve.

5. Viva la Argentina!

# AL PASTOR TACOS

My brother-in-law Brian loves to spend time in Bucérias, Mexico (it's near Puerto Vallarta), which he lovingly calls "Boos." And whenever we're there with him, we always go to Tacos Junior for a ton of these little, deeply flavored pork tacos. The pork is marinated, then layered and cooked on a large *trompo*-style vertical spit, but who has one of those? So, you can either buy one online for about $25, or MacGyver one with a pineapple and wooden or metal skewers. And these tacos are so damn delicious you must make them—but please don't let the peppers and achiote paste keep you from making them—because they're both supereasy to find online.

**MAKES ABOUT 8 TACOS**

MARINADE
4 dried guajillo chiles, stemmed and seeded
2 dried ancho chiles, stemmed and seeded
Approximately 2 cups boiling water
6 garlic cloves, peeled
½ yellow onion, sliced
½ cup fresh orange juice
½ cup pineapple juice
1 tablespoon ground cumin
1 tablespoon smoked paprika
1 tablespoon dried oregano
1 tablespoon kosher salt
1 tablespoon coarsely ground black pepper
3 tablespoons achiote paste, for color and authentic taste—you can find it at any Mexican market or online (it's definitely worth getting)

TACOS
3 pounds boneless pork shoulder
1 pineapple, to hold skewers upright (optional)
Tortillas
Roasted Tomatillo Salsa (page 33)
Diced white onion for serving
Chopped fresh cilantro for serving

1. Make the marinade: Cut the guajillo and ancho chiles into 2-inch pieces and place in a blender, add enough boing water just to cover, then cover with the lid. Do not blend; just leave for 15 minutes to soften.

2. Then, discard the hot water, but add all the remaining marinade ingredients to the blender and blend until you have a gorgeous deep red paste.

3. For the tacos, cut the pork shoulder into $\frac{1}{8}$- to $\frac{1}{4}$-inch-thick slices, then put in a large resealable bag or a bowl with three-quarters of the marinade, reserving the rest of the marinade for basting later. Mix the pork and marinade really well to make sure all the slices get covered, seal or cover, and refrigerate overnight.

4. Remove the pork from the fridge about 30 minutes before cooking, and preheat your smoker to 250°F.

5. If you have a vertical roaster (a steel spike on a stainless-steel base), sweet—if not, let's make one:
   - Cut about 1½ inches off the bottom of a pineapple.
   - Take two skewers (wooden or metal) and push their flat ends down into the pineapple base (about an inch apart) so the skewers are rising out of it.

And regardless of the type you have, this next part is the same:

1. Poke the pieces of marinated pork onto the spike or skewers, and slide down to the bottom until all the slices have been skewered.

2. If you're using a skewered pineapple, cut a small piece off the top of the pineapple, remove the peel, and fit on top of the pork, like a crown.

3. Put into the smoker and cook until an instant-read digital thermometer in the center of the pile of pork registers 145°F (this might be anywhere from 2½ to 3 hours), using the reserved marinade to baste along the way.

4. Remove from the smoker, and slice down the sides, cutting off the outside edges of the pork.

5. Add to a heated tortilla along with some of the tomatillo salsa, and top with onion and cilantro.

## Don't have a smoker?

1. Preheat to medium-high, clean and oil the grill grates, set up for two-zone cooking, and put the whole shebang on the indirect side.

2. You'll need to turn the contraption about 15 minutes so the pork cooks evenly, but you're still gonna love it!

# FILIPINO ADOBO PORK SANDWICHES

First things first—Filipino adobo is not like Mexican adobo. This is a vinegar, black pepper, and garlic version that normally is used for braising—slowly cooking meats in liquid to make them super tender and flavorful. But since this is not a book about braising, and I wanted to include it somehow, we're marinating—overnight—and then grilling. And if you make this, you'll be as happy as I was.

**MAKES 4 SANDWICHES**

Four 4-ounce boneless
  pork loin chops

MARINADE
½ cup white vinegar
½ cup reduced-sodium soy sauce
3 tablespoons light brown sugar
2 tablespoons neutral oil
2 teaspoons coarsely
  ground black pepper
4 garlic cloves, minced
2 bay leaves

GINGER MAYO
½ cup mayonnaise
1 tablespoon ginger paste or
  grated fresh ginger (but,
  honestly, ginger paste is
  a dream because fresh
  ginger is so much more
  work than fresh garlic)

TO SERVE
1 carrot, peeled and
  grated coarsely
⅓ English cucumber, coarsely
  grated, and squeezed in a towel
  to remove excess moisture
4 buns or rolls or even
  slices of bread, toasted—
  though something like
  ciabatta would be ideal
1 cup baby arugula

1. Working one at a time, put a chop into a resealable plastic bag and pound flat to roughly ⅛ inch thick. Yes, that's thin, but will be so good. Set the flattened chops aside.

2. Make the marinade: Combine the vinegar, soy sauce, brown sugar, oil, pepper, and garlic in a medium bowl and mix really well to dissolve the sugar.

3. Put some of the marinade into a small casserole dish, wide bowl, or large resealable plastic bag, then carefully add the flattened pork chops, one at a time, adding more marinade as you go, making sure they get coated well on all sides. Add the bay leaves, then cover or seal and refrigerate overnight.

4. Make the ginger mayo: Combine the mayo and ginger in a small bowl, mix well, then cover and refrigerate.

5. On the day of cooking, combine the carrot and cucumber in a bowl, then refrigerate.

6. Preheat a grill to medium-high. Clean and oil the grill grates. Slice and toast the buns first, then remove from the grill and put on the chops, discarding the marinade they spent the night in.

7. Because they're so thin, cooking them won't take long: try 30 seconds, then turn 45 degrees, give them another 30 seconds, then flip. If they need a little more, go for it.

8. Remove the pork from the grill and build your sandwiches: Spread the ginger mayo on each bun bottom, add some arugula and then the pork, and top with the carrot mixture and top of the bun. Holy crap.

# VEAL CHOPS WITH CHIMICHURRI BUTTER

Veal—how often do you have it? Exactly, and that's why this recipe is here. Veal is much lighter in color than regular beef, has a smooth texture and taste, and is more tender than beef. I find it a really nice change. Plus, it continues my quest for getting you to expand your food horizons. And, no, I don't work for the Veal Board.

**SERVES 4**

4 tablespoons (½ stick) butter, at room temperature

¼ cup red chimichurri (page 29)

4 bone-in veal chops (6 to 8 ounces each)

Neutral oil

SPG (page 20)

1. Combine the butter and chimichurri in a small bowl and mix well.

2. You can either be fancy and put the mixture in the middle of a sheet of plastic wrap, fold the top over, and roll into a log—or be pedestrian and just use it out of the bowl as I did here. Either way, refrigerate if you're not going to use it right away.

3. Take the veal out of fridge 30 minutes before cooking.

4. Lightly oil the veal and season with the SPG.

5. Preheat a grill to medium-high. Clean and oil the grill grates. When hot, put on the veal.

6. Cook, turning often (but not too often, as we want the chops nicely charred) until 140°F.

7. Remove from the grill, add about a tablespoon of the chimi-butter to the top of each chop, and tent loosely with foil.

8. Let rest for 5 minutes, then serve.

# BEEF AND LAMB

When it comes to grilling and smoking, beef is an important protein. A lot happens in this chapter, and my encouraging you to try different cuts is at the heart of it. So, be bold and try something different. The Bistecca alla Fiorentina is massive. The Caveman is dangerous—or make that dangerously fun. And Kelly's Soy & Garlic Skirt (steak) will be on your rotation after the first time you make it. There's no way you get out of this chapter unhappy, or still hungry.

## Since Beef Can Come in Many Forms, Here's a Look at Some of My Favorite Cuts

**FLAT IRON:** Well marbled, though still fairly lean, this steak is considered to be the second-most-tender after a filet. And it's actually still relatively affordable.

**FILET:** Aka tenderloin, this is supertender but with little fat, which means less flavor. That's why you often see it served with a sauce, such as hollandaise or béarnaise.

**RIB EYE:** Bone-in or boneless, this well-marbled cut with a beautiful edge of fat and intense beefy flavor should be the poster boy of "What does beef taste like?"

**TOMAHAWK:** This is the bully of the rib eye world. It's big, it's bold, and it's very impressive. And it's really just an extra thick rib eye with an extra long bone still attached. But the bone has been Frenched, meaning they've cleaned off any extra meat and fat, so it's nice and tidy and looks like a handle.

**PORTERHOUSE:** Two steaks in one. You get a filet on one side, and a New York on the other, much like a T-bone. But while a porterhouse is always a T-bone, a T-bone isn't a porterhouse. They both have the bone, but the filet is larger in a porterhouse.

**HANGER STEAK:** Once called the "butcher's cut" as they kept if for themselves. Now it's becoming superpopular because it's superflavorful and tender, but leaner than a rib eye.

**SKIRT STEAK:** Kelly's favorite, this long (I've seen them up to almost 2 feet in length) thin cut of beef loves a marinade. It's from the muscles of the cow, which means it has lots of fibers, so as always be sure to cut against the grain.

**TRI TIP:** It's interesting how many people have never heard of this cut, which is sad because it's so good. A tri tip is generally around 2 pounds, triangular, and comes from the bottom tip of the sirloin—hence the name "tri tip." But its beefy flavor is what really makes it special.

WHAT YOU DON'T KNOW ABOUT THIS PIC

TRI TIP

FILET

SKIRT

PORTERHOUSE

TOMAHAWK

HANGER

RIBEYE

FLAT IRON

# KELLY'S SOY & GARLIC SKIRT

That sounds funny, like she enjoys wearing clothing that smells like soy sauce and garlic—actually, I can think of worse things. Anyway, this is, hands down, Kelly's favorite steak. So much so, in fact, that I chose to name this simple four-ingredient marinade after her. Please note, though, I'm not calling Kelly simple, because she's not. The recipe is, even though it doesn't taste simple.

**SERVES 2 OR 3**

½ cup soy sauce

¼ cup neutral oil

5 garlic cloves, minced

1 tablespoon freshly ground
   black pepper (medium grind)

1 skirt steak (typically
   between 1 and 2 pounds)*

*If you haven't had a skirt steak, now's the time. It has great beef flavor, is relatively lean, and really loves a marinade. It's, honestly, one of our favorite cuts.

1. Put the soy sauce, oil, garlic, and pepper in a resealable plastic bag large enough to hold the steak—squoosh around well to combine.

2. Add the skirt, removing as much air as possible, seal, then refrigerate for 2 to 4 hours.

3. Remove from the fridge at least 30 minutes before cooking.

4. Preheat a grill to medium high. Clean and oil the grill grates.

5. Remove the steak from marinade and cook, turning often, until an instant-read digital thermometer reads 130°F for medium rare. Discard the marinade.

6. Remove from the grill, cover lightly with foil, and let rest for 10 minutes before cutting against the grain to serve. Let me repeat: against the grain. And because the steak is long, you'll have to cut it into small sections, turn them, and then cut against the grain. Got it?

# LAMB-STUFFED PITAS

Also known as *arayes*, these Middle Eastern stuffed pitas can be baked in the oven—but don't! Because when they get grilled face down, they become something special.

**MAKES 12 PITAS**

2 pounds ground lamb; could be beef or even a combo of the two

1 small onion, minced (about ⅔ cup)

⅓ cup chopped fresh parsley

⅓ cup chopped fresh cilantro

2 tablespoons tomato paste

3 garlic cloves, minced

2 teaspoons ground cumin

1 teaspoon ground cinnamon

1 teaspoon kosher salt

½ teaspoon red pepper flakes

6 pitas (a 6-inch pita works well for this)

Neutral oil for brushing

Garlic White Sauce (page 30) for serving

1. Preheat grill to medium-high. Clean and oil the grill grates. Set up for two-zone cooking.

2. Put the lamb (or beef, or lamb and beef; or whatever works for you) in a large bowl and add everything else except the pitas, oil, and garlic white sauce. Mix until well combined.

3. Warm the pitas in a microwave for about 10 seconds, just enough to make them more pliable so they don't rip when stuffing.

4. Cut the pitas in half and fill each pocket with approximately ¼ cup of the mixture, then flatten the pita to spread out the meat evenly inside it.

5. Brush the exposed lamb mixture lightly with oil, then place meat side down on the hot side, and cook for about 5 minutes, or until nice char marks appear.

6. Then, move the filled pitas to the indirect side and cook them flat on each side for about 5 more minutes, or until cooked through to your liking—if you shoot for 135° to 140°F regardless of lamb or beef or both, you'll be fine.

7. Remove from the grill and serve with the garlic white sauce.

# BRISKET BURGERS

There's something about brisket that just makes for an amazingly delicious burger. But because you're not likely to find it already ground in the case at the market, you're either grinding your own, or having a butcher do it. BTW, I just looked up a grinding attachment for the KitchenAid mixer on Amazon and saw them for a little as $26. Another option would be to cut the brisket into 1½-inch chunks, put in the freezer about 15 minutes, then pulse in a processor until just ground. But regardless of whether you grind it yourself or have it done— just do it. Honestly, it'll be worth it for just the smell of them cooking.

## MAKES 4 BURGERS

1 tablespoon butter

1 tablespoon olive oil

1 large yellow onion, sliced thinly

1⅓ pounds ground brisket—if grinding yourself, look for it to be about 20% fat

Kosher salt and coarsely ground black pepper

4 slices smoked Cheddar

4 burger buns

¼ cup mayonnaise

¼ cup Sweet & Smoky BBQ Sauce (page 23)

1. Preheat a grill to high. Clean and oil the grill grates.

2. Put the butter and oil in a large, grillproof pan, and add the onion. Mix well to coat, then cook in the pan on the grill, stirring often, for about 15 minutes, or until beginning to brown nicely.

3. Lower the grill heat to medium, shape the brisket into four patties, season with salt and pepper, and put directly on the grill.

4. Cook to your liking (my liking is about 135°F for medium rare).

5. When you flip them, add a slice of cheese to each patty and also put the buns on the grill—but keep your eye on both.

6. When all is ready, let's build: bun bottom, some mayo and BBQ sauce, some onion. The patty with cheese, and finally the bun top.

### If smoking:

1. You'll probably need to cook the onion inside. But preheat your smoker to 225°F.

2. After shaping the burgers, put them on the smoker and they will likely take 1 to 1¼ hours.

3. Add the cheese when they are 130°F, and pull them off when they hit 135°F for medium rare.

# MISO-MARINATED FLAT IRON

Miso is basically an umami flavor bomb—in one ingredient, it adds a wonderful savory punch. And, of course, we use it here on the flat iron, but honestly it could go on almost anything. Salmon? Yes. Pork? Yes. Shrimp? Of course. Chicken, oh hell yeah. Make the marinade, find something to put it on, and off you go. But wait—do that after making this steak.

**SERVES 4**

MARINADE
¼ cup white miso paste
   (available at most supermarkets)
¼ cup rice vinegar
1 teaspoon sugar
2 tablespoons soy sauce
1 teaspoon sesame oil
1 large garlic clove, minced finely
1 teaspoon finely minced
   fresh ginger

**Four 8-ounce flat iron steaks**

BASTING SAUCE
2 to 3 tablespoons sriracha
1 tablespoon soy sauce
1 teaspoon sesame oil

1. Make the marinade: Combine all the marinade ingredients in a small bowl and whisk until thoroughly mixed.

2. Put the steaks and marinade in a large, resealable bag, seal, and refrigerate for 4 to 8 hours (I find if I put them in the marinade in the morning, they're perfect at dinnertime).

3. Take the steak out of the fridge 30 minutes before cooking, to let it come to room temperature.

4. In the meantime, combine the basting sauce ingredients in a small bowl and mix well.

5. Preheat a grill to medium-high. Clean and oil the grill grates.

6. Remove the steaks from bag, discarding the marinade, and grill for about 4 minutes on the first side for medium rare.

7. When you flip the steaks over, brush the top with the basting sauce, cook this second side a little less, then flip and baste with more sauce.

8. Remove the steaks from the grill, brush with more sauce, cover loosely with foil, and let rest for 10 minutes.

9. Slice across grain into thin strips to serve—and if there was ever a steak that made it easy to see the grain, it's this guy . . . so, no excuses if you mess up.

# CHIPOTLE & BROWN SUGAR HANGER

Here, I am expanding your food horizons again. A hanger steak is an amazing combination of both tenderness *and* flavor—which is not something you always get. The problem is, you might not always see it at the store, so be sure to ask—or find a butcher (again) who will get you one.

**SERVES 4**

3 ounces chipotle peppers in adobo sauce

½ cup light brown sugar

1 bunch green onions

½ cup loosely packed fresh cilantro

1 cup fresh orange juice

1 teaspoon kosher salt

2 pounds hanger steak

1. Put everything, except the steak (cuz that would be gross) in a food processor or blender, and whiz until smooth.

2. Then, combine the steak and marinade in a large resealable plastic bag, seal, and refrigerate for 4 hours, up to overnight.

3. Remove from the fridge 30 minutes before grilling.

4. Preheat a grill to high. Clean and oil the grill grates.

5. Cook the steak, discarding the marinade, for about 4 minutes per side for medium rare—but definitely use your thermometer and pull around 130°F for medium rare.

6. Remove from the grill and let rest for 5 to 10 minutes before serving.

# CHILI VERDE

Make this and you'll feel like a cowboy (or is it cowperson?) in Yellowstone after a cattle drive. It's a big-flavor, beefy stew kinda thing, that's incredible with a scoop of rice in a bowl with it. Hominy are corn kernels that have been through a process called nixtamalization that swells them up so they look like corn on steroids. I know that sounds like I just made that up, but I didn't. And you can find them at most supermarkets.

**SERVES 8**

Neutral oil

3 pound chuck roast, cut into 1-inch cubes

1 white or yellow onion, diced

1 teaspoon ground cumin

4 garlic cloves, minced

One 16-ounce jar salsa verde

One 15 ounce can green enchilada sauce

One 25-ounce can hominy, drained

Kosher salt and coarsely ground black pepper

SUGGESTED SERVINGS AND TOPPINGS:

Cooked rice

Chopped onion, any color will do

Chopped fresh cilantro

1 lime, cut into 8 wedges

Tortillas

1. Put a 12-inch cast-iron pan on the grill and heat to high.

2. When it's hot, put in 2 tablespoons of neutral oil and add half of the beef. Cook until the pieces are browned on all sides, transfer to a plate, and repeat with the rest, adding more oil if necessary.

3. When all the beef is cooked and out of the pan, add a splash more oil and the onion. Cook for a couple of minutes, then add the cumin and garlic and cook until superfragrant, about 45 seconds.

4. Put the beef back in the pan along with the salsa verde, enchilada sauce, and hominy; mix well.

5. Bring to a boil and cover, lower the heat to a simmer, and cook for about 2 hours, or until the beef is super fork-tender. Season to taste with salt and pepper.

6. Serve with cooked rice, topped with some onion, cilantro, a squeeze of lime, and tortillas on the side. And trust me, whatever you do, don't dare skip the lime—it really makes it.

If after cooking you find it's more liquidy than you'd like, do this:

Mix 1 tablespoon of cornstarch with 2 tablespoons of water until smooth, then stir into the chili and watch as it thickens.

# CAVEMAN STEAK WITH HOT SAUCE BUTTER

Let me start by saying this is almost less recipe and more technique, because it's about cooking a steak on charcoal. And I do mean on, not over, like on a grill. You light the coals, and when they're ready, you put the steak directly on the glowing pile. Fun, huh? But when you do, just be sure to have people around you can show off to, cuz it's a great party trick.

**MAKES 1 STEAK, BUT SERVES 2**

1 pound rib eye—okay, you can use whatever you'd like; just make it at least 1½ inches thick

2 tablespoons butter, at room temperature

1 tablespoon chopped fresh cilantro

1 tablespoon hot sauce (I used Cholula)

A good pinch of kosher salt

Neutral oil

SPG (page 20)

1. Take the steak out of the fridge about 45 minutes before cooking.

2. Combine the butter, cilantro, hot sauce, and salt in a small bowl and mix well. Set aside or refrigerate if not using right away.

3. Light a full chimney of charcoal, and when the top is white ash, pour them into the bottom of a grill.

4. Lightly oil the steak and season with SPG.

5. Use tongs or an ash tool to make the top of the ashes as evenly flat as possible—remember, you're cooking a steak on it.

6. Then, against your better judgment, put the steak directly on the coals, and cook—and, yes, some pieces of charcoal will stick when you lift it, but you can easily knock them off.

7. Depending on the size of your steak, you're looking at somewhere around 4 to 5 minutes per side. But turn often, including just lifting up and putting back down on the same side in a slightly different spot—this will help cook it more evenly.

8. Use your instant-read thermometer, and when the temperature is where you want it, pull the steak off the charcoal (I'd yank it at 130°F), add the hot sauce butter, and tent loosely with foil.

9. Let rest for 10 minutes before devouring—which you should probably do with your hands to pay homage to our cave-dwelling ancestors (kidding).

RARE 120°

MEDIUM RARE 130°

MEDIUM 140°

MEDIUM WELL 150°

WTF? 160°

SAM ZIEN

SAM THE COOKING GUY

SAM ZIEN | SAM TH

SAM ZIEN

SAM THE COOKING GU

# Doneness

Let's talk beef temperature doneness. I've already preached the importance of a digital instant-read thermometer, but talking is one thing and seeing is another . . . so, here's what steak temps look like in real life.

But because so many factors can impact how long it takes a steak to reach your desired doneness—meat temp, out-side temp, cooker temp, how often you lift the lid, how much attention you're paying, etc.—your best chance of success is an accurate thermometer. I can't stress the importance of a thermometer enough.

I also think personal doneness is often based on looks—and if you shouldn't judge a book by its cover, should you judge a steak? Mrs. Cooking Guy (let's call her Kelly) used to turn away from a medium rare steak. But one day I had her try a few bites blindfolded of a medium steak and one medium rare, and guess what? Now she's a fan, and we're a one temp (medium rare) house. Look, I'm not saying medium rare is better, I'm just saying that, well . . . maybe I am saying medium rare is better.

# BEEF TENDERLOIN WITH BONE MARROW BUTTER

When you order a filet mignon in a restaurant, it's simply a single steak that's been cut from a whole tenderloin. So, you have a choice when cooking for a group: cook 10 individual filets, or one whole tenderloin. And I don't know about you, but I'd rather cook once and feed a bunch of people, so this is a favorite go-to when we're entertaining. Oh, and it's as tender as the name implies—but it's also pretty lean, so adding some fatty deliciousness is in order—and that's where the bone marrow butter comes in.

**SERVES 8 TO 10**

1 whole tenderloin of beef
  (4 to 5 pounds)
¼ cup prepared yellow mustard
SPG (page 20)
Bone Marrow Butter
  (recipe follows)

BTW, cooking at a low temp like this is called "reverse searing" and gives you a perfectly even level of doneness—top to bottom, side to side, and end to end. And once cooked, you'd normally give it a final sear for color. I don't think it's necessary for the smoked version because it ends up with a beautiful, dark red color. But if cooking in the oven, you might want to throw it on a hot flat top or grill for a couple minutes at the end.

1. Remove the tenderloin from the fridge about 45 minutes before cooking.

2. Preheat a smoker to 275°F. No smoker? Preheat your oven to 275°F and follow the rest of the directions.

3. You can buy a whole tenderloin already "cleaned"—which means extra fat and silver skin have been removed—it costs more per pound, but I think it's worth it. If not, just take your time cleaning it yourself.

4. Brush the mustard all over, season liberally with the SPG, and put on the smoker (if making the bone marrow butter, add the bones now).

5. Cook to your preference—medium rare is perfect, so look for your instant-read digital thermometer to hover between 130° and 135°F.

6. Remove from the smoker or oven, tent loosely with foil, and let rest for 20 minutes, then slice and serve with the bone marrow butter. But if the bone marrow butter isn't really your thing, the green or red chimichurri (page 29) will go perfectly.

(CONTINUES)

# BONE MARROW BUTTER

6 crosscut beef marrow bones,*
each about 6 inches long

Olive oil

Kosher salt and freshly
ground black pepper

3 garlic cloves, minced

8 tablespoons (1 stick) butter,
at room temperature

2 tablespoons chopped
fresh parsley

*Bone marrow is simply
the fatty tissue located
in the center of bones—
and not always, but is
usually beef. Marrow bones
come two ways—split or
crosscut. Split is cut
lengthwise and looks like
a canoe. Crosscut is cut
across and looks more like
a tree stump. Both are
great, but I prefer split—
because they're easier to
deal with.

1. Soak the bones in a large bowl of salt water overnight in the fridge—this will remove any impurities and blood in the marrow. It isn't necessary, but definitely makes for prettier marrow.

2. Preheat a smoker to 275°F.

3. Brush the cut side of the bones lightly with olive oil, season with salt and pepper, place on a small baking sheet to catch any drips, and put on the smoker.

4. Cook until the marrow is like soft butter when you poke it with a knife—roughly 45 minutes—then remove from the smoker.

5. When the bones are cool enough to handle, scoop out the marrow, use a knife to chop it fine, then put into a bowl with the garlic, butter, a pinch of salt and pepper, and the parsley, then mix really well. Alternatively, you can throw everything into a processor and whiz until blended.

6. Place on a large square of plastic wrap and roll into a log, or just leave in the bowl. Refrigerate until ready to use.

## Extra marrow? Do this:

The other thing I like to do with the marrow is to spread some on hot, crusty grilled bread, then drizzle with a bit of chimichurri (page 29) and a little sprinkle of sea salt—I can drool just thinking about it.

MULLET

MULLET IN
TRAINING

# GRILLED TRI TIP WITH SHIITAKES

Everybody loves a good "go-to"—and in the beef category, this could be it. A tri tip is reasonably priced, easy to cook, and has tons of flavor. If you've never had it, this is a good time to get your hands on one. Cuz when this delicious cut comes together with my favorite mushrooms, it's pure magic.

**SERVES 4 TO 6**

1 tri tip (about 2 pounds)

Neutral oil

SPG (page 20)

Joy's Steak Sauce (page 23)

2 pounds shiitake or cremini mushrooms, sliced

2 tablespoons olive oil

1 tablespoon butter

4 garlic cloves, minced

2 tablespoons soy paste, or regular soy sauce if you're not in love with it like me

Kosher salt and coarsely ground black pepper

1. Remove the tri tip from the fridge 30 minutes before cooking.

2. Preheat a grill to medium-high. Clean and oil the grill grates, and set up for two-zone cooking.

3. Lightly brush the tri tip with the neutral oil, season with the SPG, and put on the direct side of the grill.

4. Cook for 2 minutes, then turn 45 degrees and cook for 2 minutes more. Flip over and repeat, then move to the indirect side of the grill.

5. Baste with the steak sauce, then cook for 2 minutes, then flip and baste again. Continue to flip and baste every couple of minutes, until an instant-read digital thermometer reaches 130°F for medium rare.

6. While the tri tip cooks on the indirect side, put the mushrooms and olive oil in a large pan on the direct side (cast iron would be great here) and cook over medium-high heat until beautifully softened, 5 to 7 minutes.

7. Add the butter and garlic. Stir until fragrant, then add the soy paste and mix well. season to taste with salt and pepper, and remove from the heat until the tri tip is ready.

8. When the tri tip is done, remove from the grill, cover with foil, and let rest for 10 minutes before slicing.

9. Quickly rewarm the mushrooms and serve with the beef.

# PICANHA WITH COWBOY BUTTER

Aka "rump cap," "sirloin cap," or "culotte steak," the Picanha is hugely popular in Brazil, though not as well-known elsewhere. That's a shame though, because in terms of flavor it's about as close to the beefy deliciousness of a rib eye as you can get. It also has a beautiful fat cap and is often sliced into thick steaks, skewered, and cooked over charcoal. In fact, it you've ever been to a Churrascaria (a Brazilian steak house), you've likely had it. But we're keeping it whole and reverse searing it. Only thing is, you probably won't find it at the supermarket, and will need to get one from a butcher. Then there's the "cowboy butter." And while its origin is up for discussion, its craveability is not. Think of it as garlic butter on steroids. Huge, deep flavors that can literally go on anything. Of course, turning it into a rolled and refrigerated compound butter is certainly an option, but I prefer it still slightly warm and sauce-like.

**SERVES 4 TO 6**

One 2.5-pound Picanha roast
Neutral oil
SPG (page 20)

COWBOY BUTTER
½ cup unsalted butter, 1 stick
Zest and juice of ½ lemon
4 cloves garlic, minced
2 tablespoons finely
    chopped red onion
1 tablespoon Dijon mustard
1 tablespoon prepared horseradish
½ teaspoon smoked paprika
¼ teaspoon chipotle chili powder
¼ teaspoon crushed
    red pepper flakes
3 tablespoons freshly
    chopped parsley
2 tablespoons finely
    chopped green onions
1 teaspoon soy sauce
½ tablespoon dried thyme
Kosher salt and freshly
    ground black pepper

1. Remove Picanha from the fridge an hour before cooking.
2. Set up the grill for two-zone cooking.
3. Trim the fat cap down to approximately ¼ inch and make slices across the top of the fat (but not into the meat), about ½ inch apart, then turn and repeat diagonally.
4. Oil lightly and season both sides with the SPG.
5. Put roast on the not-hot side of the grill and close the lid. Try to keep the inside grill temp between 250°F and 300°F.
6. This can take anywhere up to about 1 hour and 15 minutes—just know you should turn the roast 45 degrees every 15 minutes to help it cook evenly.
7. When the roast reaches an internal temperature between 120°F and 125°F, turn both sides of the grill up to high and close the lid.
8. Give the roast a good sear for a minute or so on all sides to develop some charring and a little crust.
9. Remove the roast, tent loosely with foil for 15 minutes.
10. While it's resting, make the Cowboy Butter: Put all ingredients in a small pot over low heat, and combine into a glorious combination. Then let cool slightly so it's spreadable as opposed to pourable.
11. Slice the Picanha and serve with the Cowboy Butter.

# STEAK & CHIMICHURRI SANDWICHES

We've already covered chimichurri, which is possibly the one sauce steak loves more than any other. And with no shortage of steaks in this book, the chance of this combo was pretty much preordained.

**MAKES 2 SANDWICHES**

4 slices of a good bread, baguette, or even your favorite bun—you do you

12 ounces leftover cooked steak

About ⅓ cup chimichurri, green or red (page 29)

1 cup baby arugula

4 slices Manchego

1 large heirloom tomato, sliced ¼ inch thick

1. Preheat a grill to medium-high. Clean and oil the grill grates.

2. Put the bread on the grill and toast on both sides until slightly charred.

3. Cut the steak, against the grain, into thin slices.

4. Build each sandwich: slice of bread (or whatever you're using), a little of the chimichurri, half of the arugula, 2 slices of Manchego, half the steak, more of the chimichurri, half of the tomato slices, and a second slice of whatever.

5. Cut in half, eat, and be happy.

# BISTECCA ALLA FIORENTINA

This could just be the most impressive steak in the book. Bistecca alla fiorentina is a huge porterhouse prepared "Florentine style"—seasoned simply with salt and olive oil, and cooked over charcoal. This was one of the first things I knew was going in this book; I mean just look at it! Could you cook this over gas? I suppose, but should you? Let me ask you this: Do you drink Champagne out of a paper cup? Okay, bad example, because I definitely have. But the point is, to be true to it—use charcoal.

**SERVES 3 OR 4**

1 porterhouse* (about 3 pounds, or 2 to 3 inches thick; you're going to need a butcher for this, cuz you won't find it precut in the meat case)

Olive oil

Coarse sea salt

That's it.

*A porterhouse is like a T-bone, with a New York strip on one side and a filet on the other. But on a porterhouse, the filet is bigger—hence better.

1. Take the steak out of the fridge about an hour before cooking, to bring to room temperature.

2. Preheat grill to medium-high, though closer to high. Clean and oil the grill grates, and get the coals to a white ash.

3. Brush the steak liberally with olive oil, season with coarse sea salt, and put on the grill.

4. Cook for 5 minutes, then flip over and cook another 5 minutes. Then, stand the steak on its bone side for 4 to 5 more minutes.

5. If you were in Italy, it would be served rare. But since you're the master of your own domain, you can do as you please. But I beg of you: don't go past medium rare. So using your instant-read digital thermometer and knowing a steak this size will continue to cook as it rests (especially one this big), you can take it off the grill at 120°F for rare, or 130°F for medium rare.

6. Let rest for 5 minutes before cutting—and the fun thing would be to carve off the filet side and the strip side, and put them back together at the bone for serving.

7. *La cena è servita, buon appetito!* Dinner is served, *bon appétit!*

# JUST RIBS

Everybody loves ribs, and a book about grilling definitely needed a bunch of them. These rib recipes were spread throughout the book until my friend Howard asked if there were many "rib recipes in the book." And that somehow made me instantly feel like they should be in their own section—so here we are. And it now covers pork, beef, and even lamb.

# A Word about Pork Ribs, Because You'll Commonly Hear about 3 Different Types

**BABY BACKS:** Aka pork loin ribs, are called "baby" because they're shorter than their bigger spare rib relative. Each rack averages 1½ to 2 pounds, and the curved ribs are 3 to 6 inches long. But since they're more tender and more lean than spare ribs, they are typically more expensive. That being said, these are the ribs my family prefers.

**SPARE RIBS:** Considered to be meatier but less tender than baby backs. Also the bones are longer and flatter, and racks can range from 2½ to 3½ pounds each—though quite a lot is bone and cartilage.

**ST. LOUIS STYLE:** Simply spareribs that have been cut down to a uniform shape by removing the breastbone. There's more meat between the bones and they're fattier, which makes for a very flavorful rib.

## ONE MORE THING ABOUT RIBS: THE MEMBRANE.

The membrane is that white layer on the back of the ribs—you'll find it on both beef and pork ribs. It doesn't soften during cooking and keeps rub, etc. from getting through to the ribs. So, you should take it off, probably. For years, I didn't, but I do now and think it makes for better ribs. And whether you do or not is up to you, but if you want to do it, here's how:

- Look for the thin, white layer on the back of the ribs.
- Pick a rib on either end of the rack, and slide a small butter knife under the membrane at the corner of it.
- Once you manage to pull up a little bit of it, get a paper towel to give you some grip, and peel off the membrane across the rack. Sometimes, it comes off in one beautiful sheet, which is so satisfying. But other times, it's like getting the price sticker off the bottom of something you bought at Bed Bath & Beyond (when they were around)—it's one huge pain.

But there are times we want it off—like for pork ribs and some beef ribs, and times we don't, like for the dino ribs. If I think you should take it off, I'll tell you.

# PORK RIBS 3 WAYS

Because there are so many options, I'd be a mean guy if I only gave you only one way to cook ribs. So, here are three different, delicious versions, with one being a silly but crazy good homemade McRib. And there's been a running debate forever in the barbecue community on whether "fall-off-the-bone" ribs are good or bad. Some of the good ole boys feel that too tender is *no bueno*, that rib meat should have a little "pull" when you bite. So, to paraphrase that old song . . . "If tender ribs are wrong, I don't want to be right."

**MAKES 2 RACKS OF EACH; JUST MULTIPLY AS NECESSARY**

## OVEN-ROASTED AND GRILL-FINISHED

This is the first way I ever made ribs: they go from raw to finished in about 90 minutes. Are they great? Yes. Are they award-winning? If you're talking about a professional barbecue competition, maybe not. But then again, this book is not for those people. It's for the proud backyard cook. And more than a few of those have told me of their neighborhood wins. So, I suppose, yes—award-winning.

2 racks pork ribs, membrane removed (see page 163)

⅓ cup Sweet Hot Rub (page 22)

¼ cup vinegar

1 cup BBQ sauce, your pick: Sweet & Smoky (page 23), Carolina Mustard (page 25), or Alabama White (page 25)

1. Preheat the oven to 350°F.
2. Season both sides of the ribs with the rub, and place on a rack on a rimmed baking sheet.
3. Pour the vinegar into the pan (not on the ribs), seal tightly with foil, and bake 75 minutes.
4. Remove from the oven and very carefully remove the foil—there will be lots of steam and liquid—you can get rid of the liquid.
5. Clean and oil the grill grates, and preheat to medium-high.
6. Put on the ribs meat side down and grill for 2 to 3 minutes, until they develop grill marks.
7. Now, turn the ribs over and baste the top with your choice of sauce, and let grill for a couple of minutes.
8. Turn them back to meat side down to let the sauce caramelize, and baste the back.
9. Once more, flip back side down, and give 'em a final brushing with sauce before serving.

# SMOKED & WRAPPED

This is a version of the 3-2-1 method, but in about half the time—and just as good, I think. And, to me, less time cooking and more time enjoying is not necessarily a bad thing. But wait—don't stop there, because with only a little more effort, you can turn these into Your Own Homemade (But Way Better) McRib. Check out the next recipe.

2 racks pork ribs, membrane removed (see page 163)

⅓ cup prepared yellow mustard

½ cup Sweet Hot Rub (page 22)

8 tablespoons (1 stick) butter, cut into 1-tablespoon pieces

½ cup hot honey, or regular, if you prefer

1 cup BBQ sauce, your pick: Sweet & Smoky (page 23), Carolina Mustard (page 25), or Alabama White (page 25)

1. Preheat a smoker to 275°F.

2. Remove membrane, then brush both sides of the ribs with a light layer of mustard, season with the rub, then put bone side down on the grates and close the lid.

3. Leave them alone for 2 hours.

4. Take two sheets of foil, each about twice as long as the ribs, spray the center of the foil where the ribs will go with cooking spray, top with 4 pats of the butter (spaced out about as long as a rack will be), drizzle some of the honey across the butter, and then lay one of the racks meat side down on top of the honey-butter nonsense.

5. Note: If you want to make the McRib, jump down to the next recipe. If not, carry on.

6. Wrap the foil around the rack tightly, repeat with the second rack, and put both back on the smoker meat side down for 1 hour.

7. Then, carefully remove from the foil, put them meat side up on the smoker, brush them with your choice of sauce, and leave them for another 15 to 30 minutes—the goal here is to get the sauce gloriously sticky. We want them somewhere between 200° and 205°F—a little more or less is *no problemo*.

8. Then, just pull them off the smoker and serve. Sometimes, if I'm feeling playful, I like to give them a light dusting with a little more of the rub.

(CONTINUES)

# YOUR OWN HOMEMADE (BUT WAY BETTER) McRIB

Essentially the same as the previous recipe, but we let them go a little longer to get where we can literally pull out the bones.

**MAKES 3 FROM 1 RACK**

1 recipe Smoked & Wrapped Pork Ribs (page 165, prepared through step 5)

1 large egg white + 1 tablespoon water

Three 6-inch sandwich rolls

About 3 tablespoons cornmeal

½ cup dill pickle slices

½ cup thinly sliced yellow onion

1. Do everything in the previous recipe through step 5, but this time, during step 6 of that recipe, leave them on the smoker for 1.5 hours.

2. Preheat the oven to 350°F.

3. Remove the rack from the smoker, carefully open the foil, and very gently turn the rack over so it is now meat side up. The ribs will be very tender, and you could pull the bones out now—but don't—because we need them for structure.

4. Use a long spatula to transfer the rack to the smoker, brush your choice of BBQ sauce on top, and leave 15 to 30 minutes to get the sauce sticky.

5. While it smokes, beat the egg white with 1 tablespoon of water in a small bowl, brush on the top of the rolls, sprinkle with the cornmeal, then bake in the oven for 6 minutes.

6. When the rack is ready (this time, it'll be closer to 210°F), remove from the smoker and carefully pull or push out the bones, then brush again with the BBQ sauce and cut it into thirds. Now you can build: bun bottom, a little more sauce, the rib meat, pickles, onion, and bun top.

7. Booya—bite us Mickeys!

# BEEF BACK RIBS

I feel like beef back ribs are overlooked. Oh, sure, they often don't seem to have much meat on them, and unlike with other beef or pork ribs, you can see a lot of bone. But still, the flavor is insane, and when you add smoke to them . . . oh, boy. My son Jordan was here the day I was testing them, he took one bite, and just stared at them like, "Where have you been all my life?"

**MAKES AS MANY RACKS AS YOU WANT**

1 rack beef back ribs (usually 7 ribs), membrane removed (see page 163)*

Cholula hot sauce, or hot sauce of your choice

SPG (page 20)

*I like these fairly simple—with just the hot sauce and SPG. But if you wanna sauce em up, go for it. Once done smoking, add any sauce you like and leave them on the smoker a bit longer. Or in the case of the grill, let the sauce caramelize a bit over the heat.

1. Preheat a smoker to 275°F.

2. Rub, slather, paint, or even brush the hot sauce on both sides of the rack, then season liberally with the SPG.

3. Put on the smoker, close the lid, and go start *The Godfather*—it's not just timeless but about the same length as these will take.

4. After 2 hours (or roughly when Sonny gets hit at the toll booth) stop the movie and it's time to wrap the rack—your choices are either foil or butcher paper—then return the ribs to the smoker until the ribs hit 200°F to 205°F, or approximately another hour.

5. Remove from the smoker, then let rest for 20 minutes before eating—if you can wait because you're starving having sat through Clemenza showing Michael how to make his "sauce" with the sausage and meatballs.

Wanna Grill 'Em? No problem; just remember you won't get the benefit of any smoke unless you use a smoker box (see page 14). But do this:

1. Prep the ribs as described, heat a grill to medium-high. Clean and oil the grill grates, set it up for two-zone cooking, and try to maintain approximately 275°F.

2. You'll want to think about turning the ribs every 30 minutes, so they get even exposure to the heat.

3. Wrap them at the 2-hour mark, and leave them on the indirect side until approximately 205°F.

4. Remove from the grill, let rest, and consume away.

# BEEF DINO RIBS

Matt Pittman from Meat Church says beef ribs were what made him want to get into the barbecue world—and it's easy to see why. It's because beef short plate ribs are big, meaty, ridiculously delicious, and pretty darn impressive. And with only three bones, they theoretically serve three people, but the amount of beef on some can be kinda nuts, so feel free to share with more people if you want. Or can.

**MAKES 1 RACK**

1 rack of 3 beef short plate ribs (5 to 6 pounds)

3 tablespoons SPG (page 20)

1 tablespoon chipotle chili powder

⅓ cup prepared yellow mustard

½ cup low-sodium beef broth

½ cup water

1. Preheat a smoker to 275°F.

2. First and very important—please don't remove the membrane from the back of the ribs as you might with pork—because, in this case, the membrane will help keep them together.

3. Trim off any excess fat from the meat side of the ribs—some is fine, a shit ton is not.

4. Combine the SPG and chili powder in a small bowl; mix well.

5. Rub the mustard over ribs (top, bottom, and sides) and season liberally with the chili powder mixture.

6. Put them meat side up on the smoker, then leave them alone to smoke.

7. Combine the broth and water in a spray bottle, and after about 3 hours, you can start giving the ribs a gentle spritzing every 45 minutes, until done.

8. You're looking for them to get to about 205°F, or when the probe of your thermometer goes in like a proverbial hot knife through butter.

9. Remove from the smoker, wrap in butcher paper, and put into a cooler to rest about an hour.

10. Then, with everyone watching (unless it's just you and that's even better, cuz you get them all to yourself), slice right between the bones, stand back, and marvel at your work.

# CHILI CUMIN RACK OF LAMB

There's a stir-fried lamb dish from China that has cumin, peppers, and other good stuff—this is not it. But it does benefit from the chili and cumin combo, and is as delicious as it is beautiful. But yet again, I find myself thinking lamb might not be in everyone's wheelhouse, which is why it's here. C'mon . . . try it out.

**SERVES 4—IF EVERYONE WANTS 4 RIBS, WHICH I BELIEVE THEY WILL**

2 racks of lamb, frenched—means the fat and meat have been removed from in between the bone handles, and so they are much prettier

2 tablespoons chili powder

2 tablespoons ground cumin

1 tablespoon garlic powder

1 tablespoon kosher salt

1 tablespoon ground Szechuan peppercorns (optional)

1 tablespoon coarsely ground black pepper

2 teaspoons sugar

1 tablespoon soy sauce

2 teaspoons sesame oil

1. Preheat a grill to medium-high. Clean and oil the grill grates, set it up for two-zone cooking, and remove the lamb from the fridge 30 minutes before cooking.

2. Combine the chili powder, cumin, garlic powder, salt, Szechuan peppercorns (if using), black pepper, sugar, soy sauce, and sesame oil in a small bowl and mix well.

3. Brush the lamb with a light coating of the mixture. Then place meat side down on the direct side of the grill and close the lid. Cook for 4 minutes, enough to get some nice color.

4. Flip and repeat, then transfer to the indirect side of the grill, and continue to cook until you get 135°F inside.

5. Remove from the grill, tent loosely with foil, and let rest for 10 minutes, or until approximately 140°F for medium rare.

6. Then, slice into individual chops and serve with any remaining sauce mixture on the side.

# THINGS ON STICKS

There's pretty much always a dopey component to my books, and this just might be the one this time. But like I said in the rib chapter, how happy I am to eat with my hands, I'm also a fan of eating food off little sticks. But what I really like about this chapter is the variety. From the Chimichurri Shrimp to Zach's Baby Corn to the Bang Bang Tofu—ya gotta love it all. Unless you hate tofu, to which I say grow up—cuz it's effing delicious.

# CHICKEN SOUVLAKI WITH TZATZIKI

About a thousand years ago, we would eat at a tiny Greek place in Vancouver that was actually called "Souvlaki." It was right across from the beach in English Bay and we'd get a bunch of its chicken souvlaki skewers, walk across the street, eat, and watch people. Vancouver is an amazing city, but since Souvlaki is no longer there, these wonderful skewers will happily take its place.

**MAKES ABOUT 12 SKEWERS**

2 pounds boneless chicken breasts or thighs (I'd go with thighs, but that's me)

½ cup non-fat plain Greek yogurt

¼ cup olive oil

Juice of 1 lemon

3 tablespoons red wine vinegar

2 tablespoons garlic paste

1 tablespoon Dijon mustard

1 tablespoon dried oregano

1 tablespoon dried rosemary

1 tablespoon smoked paprika

Salt and freshly ground black pepper

Tzatziki (recipe follows)

1. Cut the chicken into approximately 1-inch pieces, and put in a large bowl or resealable plastic bag.
2. Add everything else except the tzatziki, cover, and refrigerate 4 hours, or up to overnight.
3. Start soaking skewers, if wooden, about an hour before cooking.
4. Remove the chicken from the fridge and thread onto your skewers. Discard the remaining marinade.
5. Preheat a grill to medium-high. Clean and oil the grill grates.
6. Grill the chicken skewers, turning often until slightly charred and cooked through.
7. Serve with the tzatziki for dipping.

# TZATZIKI

½ cup non-fat plain Greek yogurt

⅓ cup finely diced cucumber

1 garlic clove, minced

1 tablespoon chopped fresh dill, or 1 teaspoon dried

Juice from 1 lemon wedge

Pinch of Kosher salt

1. Combine the yogurt, cucumber, garlic, dill, lemon juice, and salt in a medium bowl and mix well.
2. Transfer to a lidded container and refrigerate to let the flavors really build—this will keep in your fridge for about 4 days.

# BEEF KOFTA

Cinnamon, cumin, and smoked paprika are just delicious, warm flavors that really bring these little guys together. Skewering ground beef, though, can be bit of a pain, because sometimes the meat falls off before it's cooked—so here's a workaround: shape the mixture into the small log shape but don't skewer yet; put them on the grill, cook them, and then skewer when you take them off. Or just say screw it, and forget the sticks altogether.

**MAKES ABOUT 10 SKEWERS**

1 pound ground beef

½ red onion, grated and squeezed of moisture

½ cup finely chopped fresh parsley

2 garlic cloves, minced

1 teaspoon coarsely ground black pepper

1 teaspoon kosher salt

1 teaspoon ground cumin

1 teaspoon dried oregano

1 teaspoon sumac (optional)

1 teaspoon ground cinnamon

1 teaspoon smoked paprika

Olive oil for brushing

Garlic White Sauce (page 30) for serving

Cilantro Sauce (page 30) for serving

1. Combine all the ingredients, except the oil and your choice of sauce, in a large bowl and mix well.

2. Divide into 10 equal portions and form each into a small log. Brush each lightly with oil.

3. Preheat a grill to medium-high. Clean and oil the grill grates.

4. Put the meat logs on the grill and cook 10 to 15 minutes, until they reach approximately 160°F.

5. Remove from the grill, skewer now if you like, and serve with either or both of the sauces.

# CHIMICHURRI SHRIMP

Look, once you make the chimichurri (of either color, page 29), this is a fricking snap. And don't forget, in an often high-caloric food world, these are a dream. High protein, low fat, and low calories. Look, I'm no dietitian, but you have my approval to eat a ton of them.

---

**MAKES AS MANY AS YOU WANT**

Large shrimp, 16/20's would be great, peeled and deveined (16/20 just means there's between 16 and 20 per pound)

Oil

Kosher salt and coarsely ground black pepper

Chimichurri, green or red (page 29)

1. Soak your skewers, if wooden, in water about an hour before cooking.

2. Preheat a grill to medium-high. Clean and oil the grill grates.

3. Skewer the shrimp lengthwise, through the tail first (see the pic).

4. Oil and season them lightly with salt and pepper, and put on the grill—they won't take long.

5. As soon as the first side has turned pinkish, flip them over and start brushing with the chimi.

6. Brush the non-chimi'd side as you go, and give one final brushing as they come off—they shouldn't take more than a couple of minutes total.

7. *Remember:* You can eat shrimp raw, like at a sushi bar, so you do not need to overcook them—in fact, less is more.

HOW I LIKE TO SKEWER SHRIMP

# ZACH'S BABY CORN

This is a ridiculous but delicious recipe, and one that was inspired by my youngest son, Zach—but for reasons I can't (make that won't) explain. You might remember the scene from *Big* when Tom Hanks eats an ear of baby corn by nibbling around it like a full-size ear. And while baby corn is just a younger, way smaller version of its larger cousin, you can definitely eat the whole thing. They're a little sweeter and are great in salads or stir-fries, or better yet, grilled, skewered, and served with smoked paprika aioli, like here.

**MAKES 15 LITTLE CORNS**

½ cup mayonnaise

2 garlic cloves, minced

1 tablespoon fresh lime juice

1 teaspoon smoked paprika

¼ teaspoon kosher salt

¼ teaspoon coarsely ground black pepper

One 15-ounce can baby corn (about 15)

Oil

1. Soak your skewers, if wooden, in water about 30 minutes before cooking.

2. Make the paprika aioli: Combine the mayo, garlic, lime juice, paprika, salt, and pepper in a medium bowl. Mix well, then set aside.

3. Preheat a grill to high. Clean and oil the grill grates.

4. Skewer the baby corns, brush them lightly with oil, and put on the grill.

5. You're looking for some nice charring, so turn often—this shouldn't take more than 3 or 4 minutes total.

6. Remove from the grill, and serve with the paprika aioli.

# SALMON WITH SESAME MAYO & TOGARASHI

If I had to choose only one thing to eat for the rest of my life, it would probably be salmon. It's delicious, it's a healthy protein with plenty of "good" fat, and you can cook it a million ways. When buying the salmon for this, look for as evenly cut square or rectangular piece as you can find, so the pieces will be even when you cut them. What I'm saying is, don't let them sell you the tail—it's thin, uneven, and won't be any help here. Togarashi is a Japanese pepper powder you'll find in almost any Asian market or online. And, honestly, it's worth finding because it makes so many things better.

**MAKES 8 TO 10 SKEWERS**

½ cup mayonnaise, and if at all possible, Japanese mayonnaise, such as Kewpie—it's perfect here

2 teaspoons togarashi, or 1 teaspoon chili powder plus ½ teaspoon kosher salt

½ teaspoon garlic powder

1 teaspoon sesame oil

1½ pounds salmon fillet

Toasted sesame seeds for garnish

1. Soak your skewers, if wooden, in water about an hour before cooking.

2. Combine the mayo, togarashi, garlic powder, and sesame oil in a small bowl. Mix well, then set aside.

3. Pat the salmon dry with paper towels, cut into equal-size cubes, roughly ¾-inch squares, so they'll all cook evenly, and thread onto your skewers.

4. Brush the salmon skewers well with the mayo mixture.

5. Preheat to medium. Clean and oil the grill grates. When hot, put on the skewers.

6. They likely need only a couple of minutes a side to get charred and beautiful.

7. Transfer to a plate when done, and give a light sprinkle of the sesame seeds.

# BANG BANG TOFU

Before you yell, I'm well aware that grilling cookbooks are generally filled with carnivorous dreams. But c'mon everyone, sometimes a little detour is a good thing. And it doesn't hurt that one of my favorite ways to eat tofu is to grill it. It's that combination of crispy outside, and soft inside that I love. But let's say you're not a tofu fan—Bang Bang sauce is enough to make even your wallet taste good. So, go for it—you might be surprised.

**SERVES 4 TO 6**

One 14-ounce block
    extra-firm tofu
Cooking spray
Kosher salt

BANG BANG SAUCE
¼ cup mayonnaise
2 tablespoons sweet chili sauce
1 to 2 tablespoons sriracha (maybe
    start with 1, you can always add)
Diced green onion and
    sesame seeds for garnish

1. Soak your skewers, if wooden, in water about an hour before cooking.

2. We need to drain the tofu well, so lay the block flat, cut into four equal-size slices, then lay those flat on a couple of layers of paper towels and cover with a couple more layers.

3. Cover with something flat, such as a baking sheet, then put something with a little weight—like a cast-iron pan or some soup cans from your pantry—on top of the baking sheet. The goal is to squeeze out the moisture—leave it for about 30 minutes.

4. Meanwhile, make the bang bang sauce: Combine the mayo, chili sauce, and sriracha in a small bowl, then set aside.

5. Now cut the tofu into narrower lengths or cubes as evenly as possible and thread them onto the skewers.

6. Preheat a grill to medium-high. Clean and oil the grill grates.

7. Lightly spray the tofu skewers with cooking spray, season with salt, and put the skewers on the grill.

8. Cook, turning once a side gets char marks—and when they do, you can start brushing the charred sides with the bang bang sauce. The whole process should likely be 3 to 4 minutes total.

9. When they're done (meaning nicely marked all around), remove from the grill, brush once more, sprinkle with the green onions and sesame seeds, and serve.

# CITRUS HERB VEGGIES

We all need to eat our veggies, and here's a great way to get them (plus, I needed more color in the book, because grilling food can tend to look a bit one-note). Sure, all the cutting is a bit of work, but the result is not just something so beautiful everyone will want it on their plate, but since cut veggies keep well, you can prep these the day before and get them skewered—assuming you aren't using wooden skewers. And they're kind of the ideal side dish for anything else being grilled.

**MAKES 8 SKEWERS**

### DRESSING
⅓ cup olive oil

4 garlic cloves, minced finely

3 tablespoons chopped fresh cilantro

3 tablespoons chopped fresh parsley

1 tablespoon chopped fresh chives

Zest and juice of 1 lemon

1 tablespoon honey

½ teaspoon kosher salt

¼ teaspoon coarsely ground black pepper

### VEGGIES
2 small zucchini (5 to 6 ounces each), green or yellow, sliced into rounds

2 red onions, cut into 1-inch pieces

2 red bell peppers, cut into 1-inch pieces

2 orange bell peppers, cut into 1-inch pieces

2 green bell peppers, cut into 1-inch pieces

1. Soak your skewers, if wooden, in water about an hour before cooking.

2. Make the dressing: Combine the dressing ingredients in a small bowl, mix well, then set aside.

3. Skewer the veggies by alternating among the different colors, just like the pic.

4. When you're ready, preheat a grill to medium-high. Clean and oil the grill grates.

5. Give the skewers a light brushing of the dressing, and on they go.

6. Grill, turning often (watch for flare-ups because of the oil), until the veggies are softened and charred around the edges. Feel free to liberally brush with more dressing as you go.

7. And of course brush again with the dressing when you take them off.

# JUST
# FOR THE
# SMOKER

I can hear someone already saying, "Since I don't have a smoker, I have no need for this chapter." To which I would reply:

- Only a couple of these recipes are strictly smoker dependent. And I'll give you alternative cooking methods for the rest.
- I literally just now Googled "smokers," and was shocked to find you can buy a pellet smoker for under $270—and that's amazing.

Not sure if you'll use one? Oh, you will; trust me. The first recipe in this chapter is a pork butt that you'd make pulled pork from. And the satisfaction you'll get from your very first pork butt is easily worth the $270 alone. So, if you don't have a smoker, maybe it's time to bite the bullet and go for it. Because once you've got one, the world's your smoked oyster, and the Buffalo Chicken Meatloaf, Pork Belly, and Garlic Mayo Chicken will become a few of your new best friends.

# THE RELIABLE PORK BUTT (A BEGINNER'S BEST FRIEND)

If there's anything one needs when beginning their journey into the food smoking world, it's early success—and that's why this recipe is the first one in this section—because you almost can't eff it up. A pork butt is one of the most forgiving things you can smoke. It really only needs time, and a lot of it actually, so expect this to take anywhere from 8 to 10ish hours. But the good part (other than how delicious it is) is how easy it is to prepare. Because other than some simple seasonings and a binder to help them stick, you're good.

**SERVES 12 TO 15**

8- 10-pound* bone-in** pork butt, Boston butt, or pork shoulder

⅓ cup prepared yellow mustard

⅓ cup Sweet Hot Rub (page 22)

½ cup cider vinegar

½ cup water

2 tablespoons hot sauce

*Base your per-person calculations on anywhere from ⅓ to ½ pound of pork per person, depending on what else you're serving. But also know that the pork is going to shrink during smoking, maybe as much as 40 percent.

**You can buy them boneless, but don't, because cooking with the bone in is usually considered to give you better meat. But, more important, the gratification you're going to get from pulling out the huge bone with just your fingers when it's done is tremendous. It's kind of like a "mic drop," only with a bone.

1. Remove the pork from the refrigerator about an hour before smoking.

2. Remove from the packaging and dry the pork well with paper towels.

3. Trimming is up to you, though with so much internal fat, I find the excess outside fat is not really necessary. So, I trim away any stringy pieces that might be hanging off the pork, and then if there are any superthick parts of the fat cap, I trim those down to about ¼ inch thick.

4. Preheat a smoker to 225°F.

5. First, coat the butt all over with the mustard.

6. Next, season with the rub, being quite deliberate about getting it very even all the way around.

7. Head out to your smoker, open it up, and put on the butt—fat side up.

8. Ideally we're going to cook the pork to an internal temperature of 203°F—plus or minus a couple of degrees on either side won't kill you. But we want to spritz it during the cooking process.

9. So, put the vinegar, water, and hot sauce in a nonreactive sprayer, and after about 5 hours, you can give the butt a nice spritzing, then repeat every hour and a half or so.

IMPORTANT TEMPERATURE NOTE: You're watching the temp rise steadily, and as it gets near 160°F, it stops rising, flatlines, and stays there—sometimes, for a couple hours. It's called "the stall" and the thing to do at this point is nothing—don't worry and certainly don't kick up the temp. It's going to start up again, I promise.

10. When we get to the 200°F to 205°F mark, the fat has melted beautifully and the pork will have become a fall-apart bundle of absolute deliciousness.

11. Carefully remove it from the smoker, wrap it in foil or pink butcher paper, and put it in a cooler on a couple of towels, with a couple more on top and let it rest at least an hour—but know it'll stay warm for maybe 4 more hours in the cooler if you need it to.

12. When you're ready to eat, unwrap the pork, set it in a large container, such as a roasting pan, slowly and dramatically remove the bone, then shred away.

Wrapping is pretty much like swaddling a baby in blankets. But, in this case, you fully wrap the shoulder, brisket, beef ribs, whatever, in either the pink butcher paper or foil. They both help keep in the moisture and juices, which then helps keep your meat from drying out. The biggest difference between butcher paper and foil is that foil steams more and will lessen the amount of "bark" on the outside.

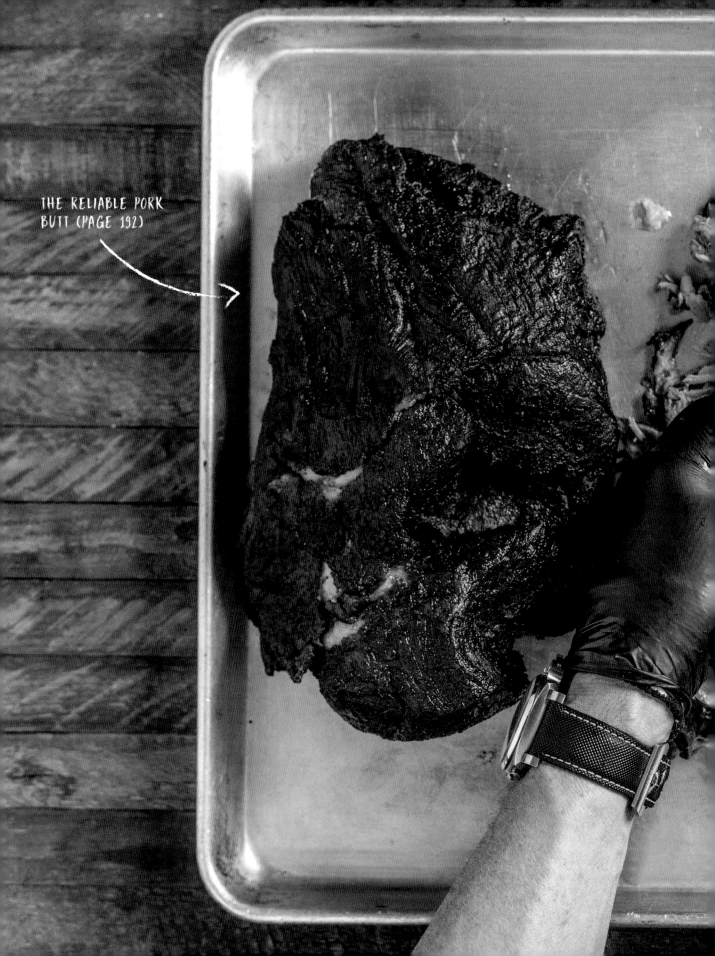

THE RELIABLE PORK
BUTT (PAGE 192)

# HANGING TOMAHAWK

Sometimes called a long-bone rib eye, the hanging part of this could be unnecessary because you could simply lay the steak on the grates to smoke it. But then a tomahawk steak is also kind of unnecessary, because there's no real benefit to the extra-long bone—other than making it more expensive because the bone is included in the price per pound. So, why then are we doing this, you wonder? We're doing it because if you have a barrel smoker, it's a fun party trick. Plus, you end up with a damn cool pic like this one—and, sometimes, we just want something cool. If you don't have a barrel smoker to hang it in, just pop it into your regular smoker and have at it, cuz you'll still get this pic. And if you don't have a regular smoker, feel free to use your grill, just see the directions that follow for that. But no matter how you choose to cook it, in the end, you get to hold up a beautiful steak like this. And it's especially beautiful because of the Chipotle Black Rub.

**SERVES 4 TO 6**

One big-ass rib-eye tomahawk (look for something 2 to 3 pounds)
Neutral oil
Chipotle Black Rub (page 22), or SPG (page 20)

1. Remove the steak from the fridge an hour before cooking.

2. Drill a ¼-inch hole about ½ inch from the end of the tomahawk bone.

3. Now, this next step is important, because the steak is heavy and has a ribbon of fat through it, and there's a chance it could literally separate from the fat and fall off the bone during smoking. So, we need to tie it up. Wrap a couple of loops of kitchen twine around the steak, just the meat, and tie it relatively snug.

4. Preheat a barrel smoker or regular smoker to 250°F.

5. Lightly rub the steak with oil, then season with chipotle black rub or SPG—personally, I think the black of the chipotle against the red of the steak is great.

6. Hang or lay the tomahawk in the smoker, close 'r up, and go chill for a bit.

7. When the steak hits 130°F, which could be about an hour and a half (so, start monitoring at about an hour in), you can pull it out—and if you want to give it a quick sear for a little crust, go for it. I definitely don't think the black rub needs it, but it's up to you.

8. Then, give it a little rest under a loose tent of foil for 15 minutes or so, aaaaand we cut.

(CONTINUES)

## On the Grill

1. If you're grilling, of course there's no need for drilling the hole, but I would tie the steak because you'll be turning it a lot.

2. Preheat one side of a grill to high. Clean and oil the grill grates, then set it up for two-zone cooking.

3. Lightly rub the steak with oil, season with your rub of choice, and place on the direct side.

4. Sear about 2 minutes, then turn 45 degrees and sear for 2 more, flip over and repeat.

5. Then, move it to the indirect side, and while cooking, flip over every 2 minutes until its internal temperature reaches 130°F.

6. Remove from the grill, tent loosely with foil, and let rest for 15 minutes before slicing.

# OLD BAY SHRIMP

Shrimp and Old Bay are a perfect match. Actually, *any* seafood and Old Bay is a pretty perfect match. And these little guys really benefit from a light smoking. BTW, this is the absolutely perfect place to use the grill basket we talked about in the "Equipment" section. The smoke definitely adds but you can grill 'em, too—just see the following directions.

**SERVES 2 TO 3**

1 tablespoon Old Bay seasoning

3 large garlic cloves, minced

2 tablespoons olive oil

2 tablespoons chopped fresh parsley, plus more for serving

1 tablespoon fresh lemon juice

1½ teaspoons smoked paprika

¼ teaspoon cayenne pepper

Pinch of kosher salt

1 pound large peeled and deveined shrimp, tails on (about 16 shrimp)*

*BTW: This would be the time to say goodbye to those shitty, pre-cooked shrimp and cocktail sauce clam shell packs you can buy from the supermarket.

1. Preheat a smoker to 250°F.

2. Put all the ingredients, except the shrimp, in a large bowl, mix well to combine, then set aside one-quarter of the mixture.

3. Add the shrimp to the large bowl of sauce and gently toss to coat.

4. Use a grill basket, or put the shrimp directly on the grates. Smoke for 15 minutes, flipping over halfway during that time.

5. Plate, garnish with parsley, and serve with the reserved sauce for dipping.

On a Grill

1. Preheat a grill to medium high. Clean and oil the grill grates.

2. Follow the directions above for mixing the sauce with the shrimp.

3. Use a grill basket or put the shrimp directly on the grates.

4. Grill the shrimp for 2 to 3 minutes per side, or until they've become pink and opaque.

5. Plate, garnish with parsley, and serve with the reserved sauce for dipping.

# SMOKED MORTADELLA/BOLOGNA

Everyone knows bologna (which we all pronounce "ba-low-nee" even though it's not spelled like that). But did you know that bologna is named after the Northern Italian city of Bologna? And before bologna (the meat), Bologna (the city) was famous for mortadella, which is quite a lot like bologna (the meat). So, mortadella started it all, and is essentially the *nonno* (grandfather) of bologna (the meat).

What's the diff, Sam? Well, mortadella is made exclusively from pork meat and pork fat mixed with seasonings. Bologna can be made from any type of meat: pork, beef, veal, lamb, turkey, chicken, etc., and then also seasoned.

And also, bologna often gets an unfair rap for being a cheap, shitty luncheon meat. I prefer to think it's misunderstood. Cold slices of it in a sandwich are okay, if not a bit boring. But when you panfry those slices first, everything changes. Now, imagine you take a big ole chunk of it or mortadella, add some mustard and barbecue seasonings, then whack it on the smoker (or on a grill; directions follow) . . . it's suddenly a whole new, and I think way more delicious, thing.

---

**MAKES AS MUCH AS YOU WANT**

1 whole chunk mortadella or bologna, as much or as little as you like

Prepared mustard, whichever you prefer (I like the version with horseradish)

Sweet Hot Rub (page 22)

1. Preheat a smoker to 275°F.

2. Using a sharp knife, score the meat by making $\frac{1}{8}$-inch-deep slits horizontally all around it—in a diamond pattern, in squares, it's totally up to you. Whatever pattern you choose, this will allow the rub and smoke to penetrate a little deeper into it.

3. Rub a light layer of mustard all over, then season with the rub and smoke 2 hours.

4. Remove, and use—any way you can think of: sliced and pan-fried for a sandwich, diced in red beans and rice, in a Benedict (oh hell, yes!), scrambled with eggs, used in a sub, or even just pieces cut and eaten right where you stand.

## Grilled Instead?

1. Set up a grill for two-zone cooking, and aim for 275°F.

2. Think about adding a smoker box with wood chips in it (see page 14); it won't quite be the same as a smoker, but is def doable.

3. After rubbing the meat with mustard and the seasoning, clean and oil the grill grates and put the meat on the indirect side.

4. This will still take a couple of hours and will require you to turn the meat every 30 minutes or so, to get it to heat evenly.

5. Then, simply remove from the grill and start using.

# BUFFALO CHICKEN MEATLOAF

We made this for YouTube and were all blown away by how fricking great it was. To start, we'd never made a chicken meatloaf before, and it was much more . . . tender, I guess, than regular run-of-the-mill beef or pork or whatever type of "red" meat–style loaf. Plus, it has the Buffalo sauce, and is studded with bits of blue cheese. And even though Kelly asked, "Well, if it's chicken, is it really a *meat*loaf?" and messed with my head a bit, here it is and I think you're gonna love it. But don't forget about the smoke, because the outside glaze just kind of soaks it in and makes it even better. You can cook this in an oven, if you like; see the directions that follow.

**SERVES 6**

MEATLOAF
2 tablespoons butter
½ medium yellow onion, chopped finely
3 celery stalks, chopped finely
2 carrots, diced finely
3 garlic cloves, minced
2 pounds ground chicken ( if you want to grind it yourself and make it ½ ground chicken breast and ½ ground chicken thighs, that would be ideal . . . but no pressure)
2 large eggs
1½ cups panko bread crumbs
4 ounces (1 cup) crumbled blue cheese
¼ cup Frank's Original RedHot Sauce
½ cup chopped fresh curly parsley
1 tablespoon SPG (page 20)

GLAZE
½ cup Frank's Original RedHot Sauce
½ cup chili sauce (not the Asian style)
3 tablespoons butter
3 tablespoons honey
½ teaspoon cayenne pepper

1. Preheat a smoker to 275°F.

2. Make the meatloaf: Melt the butter in a large pan over medium heat. Add the onion, celery, and carrots, then cook until just beginning to soften, about 3 minutes.

3. Add the garlic, stir in, and when fragrant remove the pan from the heat and set aside to cool.

4. Put the chicken in a large bowl with the cooled vegetables, eggs, panko, blue cheese, hot sauce, parsley, and SPG. Mix gently but thoroughly with your hands until combined.

5. On a large sheet of parchment paper, shape the mixture into a beautiful 12- to 14-inch loaf, then transfer on the parchment to the smoker.

6. While it smokes, make the glaze: Combine all the glaze ingredients in a small pot over low heat, and when the butter melts, mix well. Remove from the heat and set aside about one-quarter of the glaze in a separate bowl for use later.

7. You can start brushing the glaze on the top of the meatloaf after 30 minutes, and then repeat every 30 minutes until 165°F (approximately 2 hours total).

8. Remove from the smoker, tent very loosely with foil (you don't want it sticking to the glazed top) and let rest for 15 minutes before serving with the reserved glaze.

## Wanna Cook This in the Oven?

1. You can—just preheat your oven to 350°F.

2. Mix the meatloaf, form on a piece of parchment paper, and then transfer to a baking sheet.

3. Brush well with the glaze and put in the oven. Brush again every 15 minutes, or until done and 165°F.

4. Remove from the oven, tent very loosely with foil, and let rest for 15 minutes before serving with the reserved glaze.

5. And if you're wondering why the temp is so different from smoker to oven, it's because the lower the smoker temp, the longer it'll take and the more smoke flavor it ends up with.

# GARLIC MAYO CHICKEN

Everyone asks, "What doesn't bacon make better?" Well, I ask, "What doesn't *mayo* make better?" Because, outside of a few cocktails, mayo makes the world better. But just as I wrote that, I thought maybe I should Google "cocktails with mayo," and guess what . . . they exist. There's one with vodka, black pepper, Tabasco sauce, and mayonnaise. Oh, and it's a shot—does that help? And that was the least disgusting one I felt I could put here. Anyway, not that the mayo haters will believe me, but you'd never know this was a mayo-centric recipe. Only one of the "best damn chicken you've had" recipes.

**MAKES 1 CHICKEN**

1 whole chicken (4 to 5 pounds)

⅓ cup mayonnaise (I'm going to suggest Japanese mayonnaise, such as Kewpie, here, folks)

3 tablespoons Sweet Hot Rub (page 22)

5 teaspoons garlic paste, or 5 cloves, minced finely

*Spatchcocking and dry brining are not essential, but I do want to stress that they truly make a significant difference. And if you don't want to do either, I can't force you. But aren't you here to make your food world better?

1. Spatchcock the chicken (see page 74), then dry brine for at least 24 hours (see page 74).*

2. Remove the chicken from the fridge about 30 minutes before cooking.

3. Combine the mayo, rub, and garlic in a small bowl and mix well.

4. Preheat a smoker to 250°F.

5. Dry the chicken really well with paper towels, then place skin side down on your work surface.

6. Rub about one-quarter of the mayo mixture on this back side, then flip over. With some of the mayo mixture on your fingers, gently work your way under the skin on the breasts—you don't want to tear them, but to spread it under the skin as much as you can. When done, brush the remaining mayo mixture all over the skin—and that means everywhere—around the legs, under the armpits, you get it.

7. Next, simply put the chicken on a rack, then on the smoker—the rack will make getting it on and off easier.

8. Now you can take a hike; this will take anywhere up to about 90 minutes.

9. You're looking for this to land between 155° and 160°F in the breast, as it will continue to rise.

10. Then, superstar, all you need to do is take it off the smoker, tent loosely with foil, and let it rest for 10 minutes before cutting and eating.

# SMOKED TURKEY

Let me start with this: A turkey is just a big chicken, and if you can cook a chicken, you can cook a turkey. And if you can't cook a chicken, I'm here to help; just check out the Garlic Mayo Chicken (page 207). I was never a big fan of a smoked turkey until I learned a couple tricks: dry brining and spatchcocking. Those two things, done in advance, will all but guarantee turkey perfection—and, let's be honest, Thanksgiving perfection, too—because when are you having turkey outside of that holiday? Are they a little work? Sure. Do you need to plan in advance? Yup. But the payoff is a huge, smoky, delicious, and superjuicy turkey.

**SERVES 8 TO 10**

One 10- to 12-pound whole turkey, fresh or fully defrosted (little "bag o' parts" removed from the inside), dried well

¾ pound (3 sticks) butter, at room temperature

3 tablespoons chopped fresh thyme, or about 2 tablespoons dried

3 tablespoons chopped fresh rosemary, or about 2 tablespoons dried

2 tablespoon chopped fresh sage, or about 1 tablespoon dried

1 tablespoon freshly ground black pepper

2 teaspoons garlic powder

1. Let's start by spatchcocking the turkey (see page 74), then dry brine it for 24 hours to 48 hours (see page 74).*

2. Remove the turkey from the fridge 2 hours before cooking—no need to remove the salt.

3. Preheat a smoker to 275°F.

4. Combine 8 tablespoons (1 stick) of the butter with the thyme, rosemary, sage, pepper, and garlic powder in a small bowl and mix well.

5. Flip the turkey over (so it's now skin side down) and rub about one-quarter of the herb butter on this side, then flip back. Rub more of the herb butter on the skin side, being mindful to get it in every crevice, nook, and cranny.

6. Place on the smoker and cook for approximately 10 minutes per pound until an instant-read digital thermometer reads 160°F in the breast—it will be higher in the thigh—and let rest, tented loosely with foil, for about 15 minutes; during this time, the temperature will rise about 5°F.

7. While it smokes, melt the remaining herb butter in a small pot and lightly baste the turkey a couple of times throughout.

8. Then, just carve, slice, grab a leg and get into it—and remember to save the bones for stock.

*As with the chicken, spatchcocking and dry brining are not essential, but will really make a difference.

# PORK BELLY

Pork belly is simply uncured, unsmoked, and unsliced bacon. And after we shot these pics, Lucas and I stood in the kitchen, eating rich, thick, gloriously fatty smoky slices of it, talking about where else it could be used. Like in casseroles, or eggs, or salads, even chopped up and in a fried rice dish. Or the obvious—in a BLT, like the recipe that follows this one.

**SERVES 8 TO 10**

⅓ cup mayonnaise

2 tablespoons sriracha

One 3- to 4-pound piece center-cut pork belly, skin and rind removed

¼ cup Sweet Hot Rub (page 22)

1. Preheat a smoker to 225°F.

2. Combine the mayo and sriracha in a small bowl, mix well, rub both sides of the belly with a thin layer, and season all over with the rub.

3. Place directly on the grates and smoke until the internal temperature is approximately 200°F; this will take roughly 2 hours per pound.

4. Remove from the smoker, cover loosely with foil, and let rest for 30 minutes.

5. What are you waiting for? Get slicing.

And now that you have it, how about that PBLT?

# SMOKED PBLT

You can't just stand around all day eating slices of fresh smoked belly. Okay, technically you can, but you can only do that so long before it starts to feel . . . wrong. This sandwich is not just delicious, but vegetables and grains are involved to make you feel like you're doing something good for yourself. So, get to it, you health monster, you.

**MAKES 2 SANDWICHES**

Six ¼-inch slices smoked
  Pork Belly (page 210)

3 tablespoons chili sauce
  (not the Asian kind)

2 tablespoons mayonnaise

2 hoagie-style rolls

1 cup shredded lettuce

4 to 6 tomato slices

1. Heat a large pan over medium-high heat, and when hot, add the slices of pork. And whether the pork is just off the smoker or not, you'll want to do this to get the edges a little crispy.

2. As they cook, combine the chili sauce and mayo in a small bowl, mix well, and set aside.

3. Cook the belly for a couple minutes, then turn over and get the second side crispy.

4. Toast the roll, or if cooking the belly in a pan on your grill, you can put the bread right on the grates.

5. Then, build the sando: bottom slice of toast, some chili mayo, lettuce, tomato, the pork belly slices, a little more sauce, and finally the top piece of toast.

*How much to buy: If you think one bone's worth of prime rib for every two people, you'll be in pretty good shape.

# STANDING PRIME RIB

A standing prime rib is such a celebratory meal for not a lot of effort. And of course we're most used to cooking them in an oven, but once again, the smoker really ups the end product. Plus, everyone I know loves a deeply flavored, gorgeous, and supertender prime rib—everyone except my wife, that is. But she does love a rib eye, which literally comes from the center part of the roast—but she won't eat it as a roast. Don't even try to understand . . . I gave up years ago.

## SERVES 4*

One 2-bone standing prime rib (about 4 pounds)

8 tablespoons (1 stick) butter, at room temperature

3 tablespoons All-Purpose Rub (page 20)

2 garlic cloves, minced

1 cup sour cream

¼ cup mayonnaise

¼ cup prepared horseradish

2 teaspoons cider vinegar

¼ teaspoon salt

⅛ teaspoon freshly ground black pepper

1 tablespoon finely chopped fresh parsley or chives

**And, speaking of carving, remember the butcher you're becoming friends with? Butchers do this cool thing, where they cut the bones off, then tie them back on. You get the benefit of the meat cooking with the bones, but then only have to cut the strings to get them off to carve—rather than fighting with a 130°F piece of beef. And you want this because carving is much easier sans bones.

1. Remove the roast from the fridge 2 hours before cooking, to bring to room temperature.

2. Preheat a smoker to 250°F.

3. Combine the butter, rub, and garlic in a medium bowl, mix well, and spread over the prime rib.

4. Place on the smoker bone-side down and cook for 30 minutes per pound, or until 125°F; it will continue to rise about another 5°F.

5. Make the horseradish sauce: Combine the sour cream, mayo, horseradish, vinegar, salt, pepper, and parsley in a small bowl. Mix well and refrigerate (can easily be made a few days in advance).

6. Remove the prime rib from the smoker and let rest, loosely covered with foil, for 20 minutes before carving.**

7. Serve with the horseradish sauce.

You can grill instead, if you must. Follow the prep directions as above, and when ready to cook:

1. Preheat a grill to medium-high. Clean and oil the grill grates, set up for two-zone cooking, and put the prime rib on the indirect side.

2. The plan is to cook until the internal temperature of the prime rib hits 125°F and to do that evenly; you'll need to rotate the roast one-quarter turn every 30 minutes.

3. Make the horseradish sauce now, if you have not already done so.

4. When the prime rib is done, remove from the grill and let rest, loosely covered with foil, for 20 minutes before carving.

# TEXAS-STYLE BEEF BRISKET

If anything in this book is worthy of the being called the "Holy Grail," It's a full packer brisket (a full packer is a brisket with both the "point" and "flat" attached, and anywhere from 12 to 16 pounds). And "Texas style" generally refers to one being cooked with just salt and coarsely ground black pepper, period. If The Reliable Pork Butt at the start of this chapter (page 192) is a beginner's best friend because you almost can't screw it up, this might be the opposite. Not because it's particularly complicated, but more that it can be a bit finicky. So, just follow the steps and leave plenty of time. One of the biggest mistakes early brisket smokers make (as I did) is to underestimate the amount of time the whole process takes, and you end up trying to rush it, or eating at midnight. So, plan on roughly an hour per pound and you'll be close-ish. But remember: if it's done early, it can live for four hours or even longer, in a cooler, on a couple of towels and covered with a couple of towels.

**SERVES FEWER TEXANS THAN ANYONE ELSE, BUT THINK 8 OUNCES OF COOKED BRISKET PER PERSON**

One full packer brisket (12 to 16 pounds)

About ¼ cup kosher salt

About ¼ cup coarsely ground black pepper

1 cup beef broth

1 cup apple juice

## Trim

Make sure the brisket is right out of the fridge for trimming; trimming cold meat is much easier. Start by trimming the fat cap on the top down to about ¼ inch thick. Clean up the sides, including rounding off the corners; this will let the smoke and heat roll around the brisket, reducing the chance of corners burning. Some of the edges are almost all fat—you can trim these away. Flip it over and remove any extra fat or silver skin. If you're a visual learner like me, you can go to my website, thecookingguy.com, search for "How to trim a brisket," and watch it being done.

## Season

This is simple. Combine the salt and pepper in a small bowl, then transfer to a shaker, if you have one. In either case, start on the bottom and apply an even layer, then flip over and do the top—don't ignore the edges. You can let it now sit for 30 minutes to 1 hour.

## Smoke

Preheat a smoker to 250°F, and when you're ready on it goes. Remember, be thinking about roughly 1 hour per pound of brisket—so if it's already eleven a.m. or noon, you're probably not going to be eating till midnight and you'd be better off to wait and put it on at midnight, then eat the next day. In either case,

(CONTINUES)

combine the beef broth and apple juice in a squeeze bottle, and you can start giving the brisket a light spritzing after 2 hours on the smoker—and then, once an hour until you wrap it. If you put it on at midnight, don't worry about spritzing until you wake up.

## Wrap

We talked about "the stall" in the pork butt recipe (page 192); this is when the temperature of the brisket has been rising steadily, but somewhere around 160° to 165°F, it seemingly stops climbing. You literally can leave it alone because, of course, it will continue, or you can wrap it—so let's wrap. When it gets to around 160°F, take it off the smoker and wrap it tightly in butcher paper, then put it back on the smoker. Foil is an option, and can even speed up the process a bit, but it will steam in the foil and reduce the outside bark you're working hard to achieve. But, up to you. I've done both, and am cool with either. I'm also not from Texas, and not entering my briskets in competitions.

## Smoke

Reinsert your thermometer through the butcher paper and continue to smoke until it hits 200° to 203°F.

## Let Rest

Remove from the smoker, and put the wrapped brisket in a cooler, on a couple of towels and covered with a couple of towels, and let rest for at least an hour. Resting will make it even more tender and juicy—plus, it will stay hot like this for about 4 hours.

## Slice

That's it. I mean, it took a while, but here you are. You unwrap the brisket, it's still steaming, it smells and looks amazing, and now just needs to be sliced. But it would be a shame to mess it up now, so be sure to slice it . . . *against the grain*. Just know the direction of the grain changes between the flat and the point, so look accordingly.

And enjoy this most excellent of smoker delicacies any and every way you can think—which right now should just be eating gloriously delicious slices with your fingers.

# ONE DAMN FINE SMOKED BURGER

For me, in the burger world, this is about as good as it gets. Why? Well, first there's the smoke, which just adds tremendously. Then the patty of sirloin AND brisket. The combo of sautéed mushrooms and onions with vermouth is magical. And the steak sauce/mayo component is heaven. It just all comes together in a perfect sort of way.

**MAKES 2 BIG BOYS**

8 ounces ground sirloin

8 ounces ground brisket

Neutral oil

2 tablespoons Montreal steak seasoning

1 tablespoon butter

1 tablespoon oil

8 ounces shiitake mushrooms, sliced, or cremini will do, too

½ small yellow onion, sliced

2 tablespoons vermouth or white wine*

Kosher salt and coarsely ground black pepper

3 tablespoons mayonnaise

1 tablespoon Joy's Steak Sauce (page 23)

2 slices white Cheddar (because cows don't make orange milk)

2 buns (brioche, lightly toasted, would be lovely here)

1. Preheat a smoker to 250°F.

2. Put the sirloin and brisket in a bowl, gently mix together, and form into two patties; try not to overwork the meat.

3. Lightly oil the patties, and season both sides with the Montreal. Place on the smoker, either directly on the grates or on a rack on the grates—we're cooking them to 135°F, and this will take roughly 60 to 75 minutes.

4. While they cook, melt the butter with the oil in a medium pan over medium-high heat and add the mushrooms and onions.

5. Cook until they start to soften, 5 to 7 minutes, then add the vermouth, and stir until mostly evaporated. Season with salt and pepper and set aside. Resist the urge to eat them.

6. Combine the mayo and steak sauce in a small bowl, mix, then set aside.

7. When the patties hit 135°F, add the cheese to each patty, close the lid, and let melt.

8. Build: bun bottom, some of the mayo mixture, a patty with cheese, the mushroom mixture, and the bun top.

9. Have at it.

*Here's the thing: Vermouth is an excellent substitute for white wine, and once opened, is good for a few months—I would store it in the fridge though.

# SIDES

I feel about side dishes like I feel about appetizers—I want them all. My usual move at a restaurant is to suggest ordering a bunch of sides "for the table." At which point, Kelly gets mad because I'm making an assumption everyone will want them. Well, after doing a lot of research on the topic, I've come to the conclusion that Kelly is basing her comment by what she wants, and has no clue to what other people want. In short, I'm right and she's wrong. So, if we ever go out for dinner together, get ready for a bunch of sides.

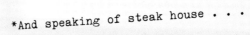

*And speaking of steak house . . .

Combine this with the Creamed Spinach with Bacon (page 231), the Hasselback au Gratin Potatoes (page 239), the Caramelized Onion & Garlic Cheese Bread (page 38), and any steak, for your very own steak house experience.

# OLD-SCHOOL WEDGE

The first time I went to a proper steak house, this was the thing I remembered most. Not the steak, not the sides (which I've already admitted to being obsessed with), but this simple, little not-so-elegant salad. It's the combination of the cold, crispy iceberg lettuce, the tangy dressing, the sharp bites of blue cheese, and the crispy panko that make it for me (okay, the panko is not so old school, but it's damn good). And then, of course, there's the bacon, which we make a little more interesting by adding pepper and smoked paprika. It's truly a classic that will be my forever start to any steak house* meal.

**SERVES 4**

8 slices thick-cut bacon
Coarsely ground black pepper
½ teaspoon smoked paprika
1 cup sour cream
1 cup mayonnaise
2 teaspoons Worcestershire sauce
⅓ to ⅔ cup buttermilk
4 ounces blue cheese crumbles
Kosher salt
1 tablespoon butter
¼ cup panko bread crumbs
1 head iceberg lettuce
1 tomato, diced
1 ripe avocado, peeled, pitted, and diced

1. Preheat the oven to 375°F and put the bacon on a rack set on a baking sheet.

2. Mix ½ teaspoon of the pepper with the paprika, and sprinkle over the bacon.

3. Bake for 30 to 45 minutes, or until done to your preferred crispness. Remove from the oven and let cool.

4. Meanwhile, combine the sour cream, mayo, Worcestershire, and about half of the buttermilk in a bowl and mix until smooth, adding more buttermilk if you prefer it creamier. Stir in most of the blue cheese (reserving some for serving) and season to taste with salt and pepper. Refrigerate; as it gets better with time, so feel free to even make it the day before.

5. Melt the butter in a small nonstick pan and add the panko. Cook, stirring often, until the panko becomes golden brown, 2 to 3 minutes. Remove from the heat, set aside, and let cool.

6. When ready to serve, remove the outer, ugly leaves from the lettuce and cut down the middle, then cut each half in two.

7. Plate, spoon some dressing over each wedge, scatter with the diced tomato, avocado, crumbled bacon, reserved blue cheese, and some of the crispy panko. Top each salad with a final few good grinds of pepper and serve.

# CHOPPED GRILLED CAESAR

This is such a simple salad that I think people forget about. And what I really love is that it starts with Kelly's Caesar dressing that's rich and a little thick as it should be—but not because of egg yolks. She cheats by using crushed croutons, and it's genius. And, of course, grilling the romaine is a huge upgrade—so the whole thing just gets better.

**SERVES 4**

¾ cup olive oil, plus
   more for grilling
Juice of 1 lemon
1 tablespoon Worcestershire sauce
1 teaspoon anchovy paste
1 teaspoon Dijon mustard
1 garlic clove, crushed
⅓ cup grated Parmesan,
   plus more for serving
1 cup The Best Croutons
   (recipe follows), plus
   2 tablespoons crushed
2 heads romaine lettuce
Kosher salt
Coarsely ground black pepper

1. Combine the oil, lemon juice, Worcestershire, anchovy paste, Dijon mustard, garlic, grated Parm, and 2 tablespoons of crushed croutons in a lidded container—add salt and pepper to taste. Close the lid and shake like crazy, then set the dressing aside.

2. Pull off and discard the ugly outer leaves of the romaine, cut a small slice off the bottom to clean it up, then cut each head lengthwise down the middle.

3. Clean and oil the grill grates, and preheat to medium-high.

4. Lightly brush both sides of the romaine with the oil and put cut side down on the grates. Grill for a couple of minutes until you get good char marks, then flip and grill the back.

5. Remove from the grill and chop into 1-inch bites, put into a bowl, add the croutons, and drizzle with the dressing.

6. Plate and top with extra Parmesan and a little pepper.

## THE BEST CROUTONS

Of course, you can buy premade croutons, but when these are sooo damn good, why would you? And if you make the Italian Canoe (page 46), you'll have the bread to do it—so it's a crouton win-win!

**ABOUT 4 CUPS**

4 cups torn bread pieces:
   French, sourdough—up to you
2 tablespoons butter
2 tablespoons olive oil
1½ teaspoons garlic powder
½ teaspoon kosher salt
½ teaspoon coarsely
   ground black pepper
¼ cup finely chopped
   fresh curly parsley

1. Toss the bread in a large nonstick pan over medium heat until it starts getting toasty, 3 to 5 minutes.

2. Then, add the butter and oil, garlic powder, salt, and pepper.

3. Continue to mix and toss until all the croutons are coated, a couple more minutes, until just starting to get crispy, then stir in the parsley. Remove from the heat, let cool, and use. They will get crispier as they sit.

# GOES-WITH-ANYTHING COLESLAW

I like coleslaw, and I really like mayo, but I do not like my coleslaw wet, as in dripping with mayo. And feel free to chop your own cabbage, carrots, etc.—I just find it a lot easier to buy the prechopped stuff.

**MAKES 6 TO 8 SERVINGS**

6 tablespoons mayonnaise

1 bunch green onions, white and light green parts, chopped finely

2 tablespoons cider vinegar

2 tablespoons sugar

1 teaspoon celery seeds

1 teaspoon coarsely ground black pepper

½ teaspoon smoked paprika

½ teaspoon kosher salt

One 14- to 16-ounce bag coleslaw mix

1. Put everything, except the coleslaw mix, into a large bowl and mix really well.

2. Now, add the coleslaw and toss superwell to combine.

3. You could eat it now, but a few hours in the fridge will make it way better.

OTHER WAYS TO USE COLESLAW

# TURMERIC GRILLED CAULIFLOWER

I originally intended this recipe to be cauliflower "steaks," which can be stunningly beautiful but are a huge pain in the ass. And that's because, out of one head, you'll get one or two perfect steaks, hardly ever three, and that's because all the rest just breaks up. So I said, screw it, let's make the whole head usable and not be a fancy boy. I'm so much happier.

**SERVES 3 TO 4**

1 large head cauliflower
⅓ cup olive oil
1 large garlic clove, minced
1 teaspoon ginger paste
1 teaspoon ground turmeric
1 teaspoon curry powder
1 teaspoon ground cumin
½ teaspoon kosher salt
½ teaspoon coarsely
  ground black pepper

1. Preheat a grill to medium-high.

2. Remove the outside leaves from the cauliflower, then cut into individual florets.

3. Combine the oil, garlic, ginger paste, turmeric, curry, cumin, salt, and pepper in a large bowl. Mix well, then add the cauliflower and carefully toss to coat.

4. This would be the best time to use a grill basket, or even a cookie rack would do. In any case, get the cauliflower on the grill and cook until softened and charred, maybe 10 to 15 minutes.

5. Remove from the grill and serve.

# CREAMED SPINACH WITH BACON

My favorite steak house side of all time is creamed spinach, so there's no way this book was going to print without a recipe for it. Besides, there's not much better than a bite of steak accompanied by a little creamed spinach. And before someone cries about fattiness from the bacon, cream, and cheese—remember, this is a shared item (at least, it should be), so don't eat it all.

**SERVES 6**

2 slices bacon, diced small

¼ cup pretty small-diced onion

Two 9-ounce packages frozen chopped spinach, fully defrosted

¼ teaspoon red pepper flakes

2 cups half-and-half

⅓ cup shredded Parmesan

Kosher salt and freshly ground black pepper

1. Put a heatproof skillet on a grill, close the lid, and heat to medium-high.

2. Add the bacon and cook until about three-quarters of the way done and, while leaving the bacon in the pan, remove all but a couple of tablespoons of the grease.

3. Put in the onion and cook for 5 minutes, or until softened.

4. Spread out a large, clean kitchen towel, put the defrosted spinach in the center of it, fold up the sides, and squeeze like you mean it, until you get out as much liquid as you can.

5. Now, add the spinach and red pepper flakes to the pan and mix well with the bacon and onion, breaking up the spinach clump.

6. Pour in the half-and-half and stir well to combine everything.

7. Add the Parmesan and season with salt and pepper to taste.

8. Continue to cook until thickened and stupidly delicious.

# PULLED PORK EGG ROLLS

You already made your pulled pork for The Reliable Pork Butt recipe (page 192), so now let's use some of it for this nice change up to basic egg rolls.

**MAKES ABOUT 12 EGG ROLLS**

1 pound pulled pork (page 192)

3 to 4 tablespoons Sweet & Smoky BBQ Sauce (page 23)

1½ cups Goes-with-Anything Coleslaw (page 227)

1 cup shredded Monterey Jack

1 large egg + 1 tablespoon water

12 egg roll wrappers

Vegetable oil for frying

Honey Mustard Sauce (recipe follows)

And btw, you could absolutely cook these on your stove inside—but this is a grilling book. Never forget a grill can really be used as an oven and a stove, it's just outside!

1. Put the pork, BBQ sauce, coleslaw, and cheese in a large bowl and mix well.

2. Beat the egg with the water in a small bowl and set aside.

3. Lay an egg roll wrapper on the counter, with a point facing you. Place approximately ¼ cup of the coleslaw mix on the lower third of the wrapper, then fold the point over the filling, snugging the wrapper back toward you slightly as it encloses the filling, to make a tighter tube.

4. Now, fold each side in toward the middle and brush a little of the egg wash on the farthest point. Finish by rolling it away from you, making sure to press to seal up the seam.

5. Repeat until all 12 wrappers are filled and rolled.

6. Put a couple of inches of vegetable oil in a large cast-iron pan, then place on the grill, and heat to 350°F.

7. Add the egg rolls, four or five at a time so as not to overcrowd them, and cook until golden on all sides, 3 to 4 minutes.

8. Drain on paper towels, and serve with the honey mustard sauce.

## HONEY MUSTARD SAUCE

¼ cup stone-ground mustard, or any you prefer . . . maybe not basic yellow, though

3 tablespoons honey

1 tablespoon cider vinegar

2 teaspoons smoked paprika

1 tablespoon finely chopped fresh cilantro

½ teaspoon kosher salt

Combine all the ingredients in a small bowl and mix well.

# FRENCH ONION MAC & CHEESE

Is this strictly a grilling recipe? No. So, why is it in here? Because any book filled with a ton of grilled meats needs a good side of mac. Plus, this has all the flavor and deliciousness of French onion soup, only it's a creamier, richer version—and who could complain about that? Here's the perfect time to pull out your large cast-iron pan.

**SERVES 6**

2 tablespoons butter

2 pounds yellow onions, sliced thinly

Kosher salt and coarsely ground black pepper

Leaves from 4 or 5 thyme sprigs

1 pound dried pasta—a tube shape, such as penne, will hold the sauce better

¼ cup vermouth

1 large garlic clove, minced

1 cup beef broth

1 cup heavy cream

8 ounces shredded Gruyère

4 ounces shredded white Cheddar

1½ to 2 ounces crispy fried onions, the kind you use at Thanksgiving

1. Heat a grill to medium high, put on a 10- to 12-inch heatproof pan, and when hot, add the butter and onions. Cook, stirring well, for a couple of minutes.

2. Season lightly with salt and pepper, then add the thyme. Mix well and continue to cook, stirring often, until the onions are beautifully browned, 20 to 25 minutes.

3. This is the perfect time to boil your pasta (okay, you'll probably go inside to do this—is that asking so much?). Oh, and don't overcook—keep them al dente.

4. Add the vermouth to the onion mixture and stir, scraping along the bottom to get up the fond (browned bits) and when mostly evaporated, add the garlic. When fragrant, pour in the beef broth and cream. Stir well and let cook until slightly thickened.

5. Combine the Gruyère and Cheddar in a bowl and mix well.

6. Add the cooked pasta to the pan, stir well, and slowly start adding the cheese mixture—if you add too fast, it will just be a big, clumpy ball—holding back about half of the mixture.

7. When nicely melted and combined, top with the remaining cheese and finally the crispy onions, and close the lid until just melted.

8. Serve.

# TEMPURA ONION RINGS

There's just something right about a good, crispy onion ring alongside grilled food. And remember this: once most things are grilled relatively hot and fast, they'll need to rest for 10 to 20 minutes before eating, and that's the perfect time to make these. Have the onions cut, floured, and waiting to be dipped and fried. Then, take off your steak, chicken, whatever, and off you go.

**MAKES ABOUT 20**

2 yellow onions

1½ cups all-purpose flour

½ cup cornstarch

Kosher salt

1 teaspoon smoked paprika

1 teaspoon garlic powder

¼ teaspoon coarsely ground black pepper

½ teaspoon baking powder

12 ounces beer—up to you what kind, bucko

Vegetable oil for frying

1. Cut off and discard the top and bottom ½ inch of the onions, peel, then cut into ½-inch-thick slices, separate into rings, and set aside.

2. Combine ½ cup of the flour and the cornstarch in a large bowl and add 1 teaspoon of salt plus the paprika, garlic powder, pepper, and baking powder.

3. Mix well, then slowly whisk in the beer until relatively smooth; it should be like a thin pancake batter.

4. Put the remaining cup of flour in another bowl.

5. Pour a couple of inches of vegetable oil in a large cast-iron pan, place on your grill, and heat to roughly 375°F over medium-high heat.

6. When ready, toss the onions in the plain flour to coat, knock off any excess, then dip into the batter, also shaking off the excess.

7. Cook four or five at a time in the pan (you don't want to overcrowd) until golden brown, 2 to 3 minutes.

8. Transfer to a baking sheet, sprinkle with a little more salt, and serve.

MORE WAYS TO ENJOY ONION RINGS

# HASSELBACK AU GRATIN POTATOES

Meat and potatoes, right? There's no way anyone will be mad when you bust these out to accompany some ribs, steak, or anything else in this book. And if making the potatoes all pretty by having them stand up is more work than you want, just lay 'em down like regular scalloped or au gratin potatoes—because they'll definitely eat the same way.

**SERVES 8 TO 10**

- ⅓ pound (5.3 ounces) bacon, chopped finely
- ½ large yellow onion, diced finely
- 2 ounces grated smoked Gruyère
- 2 ounces grated fontina
- 2 ounces grated Parmesan
- 2 cups heavy cream
- 3 garlic cloves, minced
- 2 teaspoons fresh thyme leaves
- 2 teaspoons kosher salt
- 1 teaspoon coarsely ground black pepper
- 4 pounds russet potatoes
- 2 tablespoons butter

1. Preheat a smoker or oven to 400°F; if using a grill, preheat to medium-high and set up for two-zone cooking.

2. Place the bacon in a small pan and cook until about halfway done. Remove any excess grease and add the onion. Cook for about 5 minutes more, or until the onion is beginning to soften. Remove from the grill and set aside to cool slightly.

3. Combine the three cheeses in a large bowl, then set aside about 1/3 cup of the mixture. To the cheese in the large bowl, add the cream, garlic, thyme, salt, pepper, and the now-cooled bacon and onion mixture. Mix well.

4. Slice the potatoes about $\frac{1}{8}$ inch thick (I used a mandoline), and as you do so, put them into the bowl that contains the cream mixture. Gently (so you don't break them), toss the slices so they all get coated.

5. Butter the bottom of a 9-by-12-inch casserole dish, and put in the potato slices, standing them up as best you can, until they're all in.

6. When you're done, pour any remaining cream from the bowl over the top, cover tightly with foil, put on a baking sheet in case it spills over, and smoke or bake for 45 minutes.

7. Remove the foil, sprinkle the reserved cheese over the top, and continue cooking another 30 to 45 minutes, or until gorgeously brown and bubbly.

8. I'd let sit a few minutes before you serve—if you have the willpower.

# DRINKS
# AND
# DESSERTS

Full disclosure: I'm not a big dessert guy, though I can appreciate a bite or two of something sweet after a meal. But this book isn't for me, it's for you guys, and you guys love your desserts.

CHELADA (CON TEQUILA)

MICHELADA

# MICHELADA

A beer while cooking outside just seems right as rain. Wait, is that a messed-up expression? Because outside of a forest fire, or lazy Sunday morning, when is rain a good thing—no? But a few extra ingredients make it so much more.

**MAKES 1 DRINK**

Regular salt or a chili lime salt (such as Tajín) for the rim

Lime wedge

4 ounces Clamato juice

Juice of 1½ limes

1 teaspoon soy sauce or Worcestershire sauce (my pref would be soy)

1 teaspoon hot sauce (I'm going with Cholula)

12 ounces Mexican lager

1. On a small plate, make an even layer of salt.
2. Wet the rim of a glass with the lime wedge, and dip the glass evenly into the salt.
3. Then, add the Clamato, lime juice, soy sauce, and hot sauce.
4. Stir well to mix, add some ice and the beer, and finally, squeeze and drop in the lime wedge.

# CHELADA (CON TEQUILA)

Think of this as the superrefreshing but lazy version of a Michelada. I suppose you could use Tajín on the rim here, too—but I like just salt for this. And I suppose the tequila could be optional, but it shouldn't be.

**MAKES 1 DRINK**

Kosher salt

Lime wedge

Juice of 1½ limes

12 ounces Mexican lager

1½ ounces blanco tequila (optional)

1. On a small plate, make an even layer of the salt.
2. Wet the rim of a glass with the lime wedge, and dip the rim evenly into the salt.
3. Add the lime juice, beer, and the not-optional tequila.
4. Add ice, stir, then squeeze and drop in the lime wedge.

# ANGEL FOOD CAKE WITH CHOCOLATE SAUCE & GRILLED PINEAPPLE

I'm going to make this supereasy for you, because we're starting with a store-bought cake.

**SERVES 16**

CHOCOLATE SAUCE*
3 tablespoons butter
2 ounces unsweetened
  chocolate (I use Baker's)
6 ounces evaporated milk
¾ cup sugar

1 fresh pineapple
1 store-bought angel food cake
Toasted almonds for garnish
Simple Raspberry Sauce
  (page 251; optional)

*I put the unused chocolate sauce in a freezer container. Then, when I need it, I microwave it on LOW until melted. In fact I always have some in the freezer.

1. Make the chocolate sauce: Combine the butter and chocolate in a small pot over low heat and stir until melted, then stir in evaporated milk and slowly add the sugar.

2. Bring to a low boil and cook for 2 to 3 minutes, stirring often, then remove from the heat and set aside.

3. Cut the top and bottom off the pineapple, stand it up, then carefully cut down along the sides to remove the rind.

4. Then, cut straight down, to get approximately ½-inch thick slices of pineapple—they'll be perfect for grilling.

5. Preheat a grill to medium-high. Clean and oil the grill grates.

6. Slice the angel food cake into as many wedges as you need—you'll get about 16 out of a whole cake.

7. Put as many pineapple slices as you need on the grill, and cook on both sides until nicely charred.

8. As you take them off, clean and oil the grill grates again and put on the cake slices.

9. Cook until marked, but know these will grill fast, as in maybe a minute or so per side.

10. Remove the cake from the grill and serve with the pineapple, drizzled with the warmed chocolate sauce and garnished with almonds.

## Let's Talk about Grilling Fruit

Why? Because it's kind of sensational. They soften, they sweeten up a bit more, and the charring just adds a ton of greatness and looks! My favorites to grill are pineapple and any stone fruit (peaches being my favorite), pears, bananas are fun, and avocado is wonderful—and, yes, avocados are technically a fruit, not a vegetable.

You essentially have three choices for how to grill:

1. Large pieces that won't fall through can go directly on the cleaned and oiled grates,
2. Smaller pieces can be skewered, or
3. You can use a grill basket.

And there's no need to overthink it. Even just a big bowl of beautifully grilled fruit put in the center of the table after dinner will make everyone happy.

# THE BEST THING TO DO WITH ICE-CREAM SANDWICHES

You've smoked, grilled, and barbecued. Everyone is full and happy. But wouldn't a little bite or two of something sweet be wonderful? Then, you remember that I told you to keep ice-cream sandwiches in your freezer . . . and in a few minutes, you bring this guy out. Your guests grab one of the triangles, drag it through the extra chocolate and smashed mint cookies, and voilà—you're an instant hero.

**PROBABLY SERVES 4 OR 5**

4 ice-cream sandwiches

¼ cup Chocolate Sauce (page 244), not hot, just pourable

4 chocolate mint cookies (Girl Scout Thin Mints are perfect), frozen and smashed up

1 tablespoon powdered sugar

1. Slice the ice-cream sandwiches in half to make two mini sandwiches, then slice each half diagonally so you wind up with four triangles.*

2. Stand up the triangles in an interesting way on a plate, drizzle with some chocolate sauce, add the crumbled cookies over the top, and give a final shake of the powdered sugar. Talk about edible art!

*I like to cut the sandwiches in advance and have them lined up all pretty on the serving plate and in the freezer. It makes the whole process faster at dessert-time, plus they can start melting during the cutting, and that's no fun.

*We shot the photos for the book in February, and fresh peaches were not available. But frozen were, and after defrosting them, drying them on paper towels, and making them into the pie—you never would have known. So, that means you can make this all year round.

# GRILLED PEACH & RASPBERRY PIE

Let me set the stage for you, Bud (my family in Canada all call one another Bud): You've just grilled the Garlic Mayo Chicken (page 207), the grill is still hot, so why not use it to cook a pie? The Chinese expression for it (spelled phonetically, of course) is "eeshou errnow." And it means "two birds, one stone." I think. Either that or I just said something really bad.

**SERVES 6**

2 ripe peaches,* sliced into 12 to 16 wedges each (no need to peel), or the equivalent of defrosted (previously frozen) peach slices

6 ounces raspberries

1 to 2 tablespoons sugar, depending on how sweet your fruit is

3 tablespoons all-purpose flour

Zest of 1 lemon

1 store-bought uncooked piecrust (the kind that you can unroll and lay flat)

1 large egg, beaten

Turbinado sugar for sprinkling**

Serve with Boozy Whipped Cream and/or Simple Raspberry Sauce (recipes follow)

**And before you accuse me of going full Martha Stewart, you'll know turbinado sugar by its more popular retail name, Sugar in the Raw, that caramel-colored, chunkier sugar in the brown packet you'll find at many coffee shops. I like it because it's more noticeable on the pie, plus it adds a slight crunch.

1. Preheat a grill to medium-high. Clean and oil the grill grates, and set up for two-zone cooking.

2. Combine the peaches, raspberries, sugar, half of the flour, and lemon zest in a medium bowl and mix carefully so you don't mash up the fruit.

3. Fold about a 2-foot-long piece of aluminum foil in half and place on the counter. Dust with the remaining flour, and roll out the piecrust on top.

4. Place the fruit mixture in the middle of the crust, leaving about a 2-inch bare border all around.

5. Then, fold the border in and up, with a series of pleats, not to cover the fruit, but to come a couple of inches up as a sort of tartlike rim.

6. Brush the exposed dough rim with beaten egg and sprinkle with the turbinado sugar.

7. Place the pie, with the foil underneath on the indirect side of the grill.

8. Close lid and cook, giving the pie a quarter turn every 10 minutes or so, until the exposed crust is beautifully golden brown, 25 to 30 minutes.

9. Bring to the table, and serve with the boozy whipped cream or simple raspberry sauce—or both.

# BOOZY WHIPPED CREAM

Just so you know, 1 cup of heavy cream will make enough whipped cream to top roughly 8 to 10 slices of pie. So make as much as you want, or need.

1 cup heavy cream

1 ounce bourbon, or see the sidebar for other ideas

Combine the cream and bourbon in the bowl of a stand mixer fitted with the whisk attachment or just a large bowl (use a hand mixer or, if you are feeling athletic, a large whisk). Beat until thick.

And once you know how a little bourbon can impact your whipping cream, you should try other things. Give these a shot:

**Almond tequila**—It's a little like amaretto, and would be amazing on a lot of things.

**Grand Marnier**—A little orangey, a little sweet, all good; would be nice on apple pie.

**Chambord (raspberry liqueur)**—This is so good, especially with fresh berries, too.

**Coconut rum**—On top of some beautifully grilled peaches is one of my favorites.

**Vodka**—In whipping cream, this is bad, very bad—so don't even think it.

# SIMPLE RASPBERRY SAUCE

This is one of my favorite things in the book. And considering it's one of only a few "not grilled" items in a book dedicated to grilling, that's saying a lot.

**MAKES ABOUT 2 CUPS**

2 tablespoons water

12 ounces fresh or frozen raspberries (roughly 2 cups)

Zest and juice of ½ lemon

2 tablespoons sugar, or to taste (depending on how sweet the berries already are, and how sweet you like this, cuz I prefer it not too sweet)

1 tablespoon cornstarch + 2 tablespoons water

1. Heat a small saucepan over medium heat and add the water, half of the raspberries, the lemon zest and juice, and the sugar.

2. Stir well to combine, allowing the mixture to simmer and break down the berries over the next 5 to 7 minutes, stirring and mashing some of the berries as you go.

3. Add the remaining berries, squishing a little more as you put them in, then continue to simmer for another 5 minutes.

4. If you like it thicker, mix the cornstarch and water to make a smooth slurry, then start by stirring about half of it into the sauce. If it's thick enough for you, move on. If not, stir in remaining slurry.

5. Remove from the heat, let cool, and store in the refrigerator.

# THE BEST BANANAS FOSTER

Bananas Foster is a very old-school, tableside preparation you almost never see anymore. And I normally wouldn't like something like it, but when the bananas are grilled and get all charred up, and banana ice cream and banana chips are added, it's really damn great.

**SERVES 4**

4 tablespoons (½ stick) butter

2 slightly firm bananas, not too hard but not soft ripe

¼ cup light brown sugar

¼ cup dark rum

4 scoops banana ice cream (this is not a promo, but Ben & Jerry's Chunky Monkey is insane here)

½ cup dried banana chips, crushed slightly

1. Preheat a grill to medium. Clean and oil the grill grates.

2. Put the butter in a medium grillproof skillet and set on the grill.

3. Leaving the peel on, slice the bananas lengthwise, brush the cut sides with the now melting butter, and place, face down, on the grill.

4. Your goal over the next 3 to 4 minutes is to get the bananas grilled up really well. Don't worry if you think it's too much; you're doing only one side.

5. While they grill, add the brown sugar to the remaining butter and mix well to combine.

6. When the bananas are done, transfer them to a plate, remove the peel, and cut the fruit into ¾-inch bites. Add them to brown sugar mixture.

7. Gently mix to coat, then remove from the heat, add the rum, and—away from your face and body—use either a kitchen torch or lighter to carefully ignite the rum . . . it'll go out quickly on its own.

8. Plate and serve with ice cream and some of the banana chips, and drizzling with the pan sauce.

# INDEX

Note: Page references in *italics* indicate photographs.